PEDIATRIC EARLY ELEMENTARY EXAMINATION

Peex 2

Examiner's Manual

Developed under the direction of
Melvin D. Levine, MD, FAAP

From
The Division of Ambulatory Pediatrics
and The Middle Childhood Project,
The Children's Hospital, Boston, MA.

Further developed by
Melvin D. Levine, MD, and Adrian D. Sandler, MD,
at the Clinical Center for the Study of Development and
Learning, University of North Carolina at Chapel Hill,
and supported in part by a grant from the
Robert Wood Johnson Foundation.

Educators Publishing Service, Inc.
Cambridge and Toronto

Cover design by Joyce Weston
Illustrations by Anne Lord

Dr. Mel Levine is Director, The Clinical Center for the Study of Development and Learning (a university-affiliated program) at the University of North Carolina at Chapel Hill, and Professor of Pediatrics, University of North Carolina School of Medicine.

Dr. Adrian Sandler is Medical Director, The Olson Huff Center for Child Development, Thoms Rehabilitation Hospital, Asheville, North Carolina.

September, 1996 Printing

Acknowledgments

The creation of the *PEEX 2* has been made possible through the collaboration of many dedicated and knowledgeable professionals who have worked either on the current edition or the initial version. The following people contributed their ideas and their time.

For the original *PEEX*:

Dr. Elizabeth Wiig

Dr. Lynn Meltzer

Dr. Barry Zallen

Dr. Betsy Busch

Dr. Terrence Fenton

Edward Maroney

Dr. Leonard Rappaport

Dr. Frank Oberklaid

Carey Aufseeser

Dr. Janice Lowe

Dr. Paula Menyuk

For the *PEEX 2*:

Dr. Katherine Butler

Dr. Stephen Hooper

Dr. James Montgomery

Martha Reed

Dr. Linda Siegel

Dr. Virginia Berninger

Tim Brown

Barbara Cassell

Dr. Lynn Wegner

Dr. Paula Menyuk

Dr. Marc Ruggiero

Dr. Cynthia Steinem

We would also like to acknowledge a group of practicing pediatricians who offered practical suggestions and collected normative data on the *PEEX 2*.

Dr. Alice Kozner

Dr. Stephen Koffler

Dr. Robin Smith

Dr. Mark Roth

David Evans

Dr. Bruce Pasch

Dr. Kuldip Malhotra

Dr. Betty Wolf

Dr. Martin Hoffman

Support for the development of this examination was provided by the Robert Wood Johnson Foundation, Princeton, New Jersey, and by the Administration for Developmental Disabilities and the U.S. Maternal and Child Health Bureau.

Contents

Introduction

This *Examiners Manual* is a guide to administration and interpretation for clinicians using the *Pediatric Early Elementary Examination 2*, a completely revised edition of the original *PEEX*. The *PEEX 2* is a neurodevelopmental examination for children between the ages of six and nine. It enables health care and other professionals to derive an empirical description of a child's development and functional neurological status. As such, the *PEEX 2* is more comprehensive than a developmental *screening* test, but it does not yield a total or definitive evaluation of function in any *particular* area. In most instances, the *PEEX 2* is used to evaluate children about whom there are some concerns. The results can help identify those areas of developmental function that merit further and more specific assessments or provide a pediatric neurodevelopmental perspective in conjunction with the observations of other professionals during multidisciplinary evaluations.

The *PEEX 2* does not yield an overall score or diagnostic label. Rather, it contributes to the development of a descriptive profile of a child's strengths, weaknesses, and current ways of learning. Such a profile can have significant implications for educational planning, counseling, the use of medication, and the enhancement of strengths.

The minds of children between the ages of six and nine undergo an accelerated period of development. Newly acquired capabilities of their minds are crucial to learning basic academic skills and how to use learning strategies. Among the many areas of rapid growth are children's abilities to process and use the sounds that comprise their language, to acquire vocabulary, to utilize various components of memory effectively, to become increasingly planful and selective in their attention, to begin using effective strategies to complete tasks, and to communicate with precision and fluency. When children fail to advance in these and other critical areas of development, their educational experience can become a source of constant frustration and humiliation. At the same time, they can fall behind in attaining a range of important academic subskills and skills. Fortunately, such children can be helped effectively when the reasons for their difficulty are well understood. The *PEEX 2* is an instrument that has been designed to help facilitate such understanding.

The Evolution of the *PEEX 2*

The *PEEX 2* is one of a series of neurodevelopmental examinations developed by Dr. Mel Levine and his colleagues in North Carolina and previously in Boston. Younger children are evaluated on the *Pediatric Extended Examination at Three (PEET)* (ages three to four) and the *Pediatric Examination of Educational Readiness (PEER)* (ages four to six). Older students undergo evaluation on the *Pediatric Examination of Educational Readiness at Middle Childhood 2 (PEERAMID 2)* (ages nine to fifteen).

The development of these neurodevelopmental assessments has been an ongoing process since the early 1970s and one that is continually subject to revision and improvement. As the field of learning disorders and the study of neurodevelopmental function advance, so the assessments must be adapted to reflect these developments. In 1992 a planning grant, part of which was designated to refine the *PEEX* and the *PEERAMID* to make them more useful to pediatricians and other professionals who are interested in school problems and learning disorders, was obtained from the Robert Wood Johnson Foundation. The *PEEX 2* and *PEERAMID 2* are the results of this process.

Readers who are familiar with the original *PEEX* will recognize the majority of the contents of the *PEEX 2*. Some tasks have been added, based on evidence from recent research indicating the need to tap into specific functions that were not represented previously. For example, we have included a substantial section on phonology since it is becoming increasingly evident that phonological awareness and processing contribute significantly to the acquisition of skills for decoding words in early elementary school. The *PEEX 2* also includes more emphasis on various forms of memory, as it has been demonstrated that even subtle dysfunctions of mnemonic ability can have serious negative impacts on knowledge and acquisition of skills. These tasks have been pilot tested prior to inclusion in the *PEEX 2*.

The format of the *PEEX 2* has been altered so that it now more closely resembles the *PEERAMID 2*. This modification resulted from a consensus among users of both examinations that somehow the original *PEERAMID* was more user friendly than was the original *PEEX*.

Some sections of the *PEEX 2* have been reduced in length. Language tasks have been shortened. There is less stress on temporal-sequential organization, and sequencing items have been subsumed mainly under memory. Visual recognition tasks have been replaced by a more extensive assessment of visual processing. Within the fine motor section, there is a somewhat greater emphasis on praxis. The gross motor section remains essentially intact.

This process of revision was undertaken systematically, using the following methods. First, we considered the results of validity studies that examined factor structure of the original *PEEX* and concurrent relationships with other measures. Through these statistical methods, it was possible to develop a clearer sense of how individual tasks were related and which functions they were actually measuring. Those tasks that did not appear to have validity and that extensive clinical experience could not support were eliminated. Some of these changes, although regrettable, were felt to be in the interest of developing an outstanding and supportable instrument. Although published data on the neurodevelopmental tests are as yet limited, relevant references are provided at the end of this manual.

Second, feedback was obtained from many clinicians all over North America about their experiences with these instruments. Wherever possible, their comments and suggestions were taken into account in the revision process. Third, several nationally-renowned experts were consultants on the content of the instruments and their input was incorporated into the *PEEX 2*.

As with previous neurodevelopmental examinations, the *PEEX 2* represents one contribution to a multifocal assessment process and is not intended to be used in isolation. The *PEEX 2* does not yield an overall score or even subtest scores. Instead, the examination is designed to help generate a narrative description of a child's neurodevelopmental profile. Success or failure on any particular item can have multiple possible causes. Therefore, the process of task analysis and the search for recurring themes (both within the *PEEX 2* and beyond it) are at the heart of the diagnostic algorithm. The *PEEX 2*, like other neurodevelopmental examinations, provides an opportunity to spend about an hour with a child in order to record developmentally appropriate systematic observations. At the same time that we are noting various successes and failures on a range of tasks, we are also trying to make reliable observations of behavior, affect, attention, and the use of strategies. The *PEEX 2* is administered with a complete physical, sensory, and neurological examination. It is intended to be supplemented with *The ANSER System Parent* and *School Questionnaires* as well as with other available historical or concurrent data and the results of any prior testing.

General Information

Duration

The *PEEX 2* takes approximately one hour to administer.

Terminology and Task Analysis

In order to avoid confusion over terminology, we have developed a set of constructs and their component elemental functions that we use consistently throughout both the *PEEX 2* and the *PEERAMID 2*. These are shown in the task analysis pages, which can be found toward the end of the *Record Form*s. As a guide to examiners, this information is listed in boxes in the upper right-hand corner of each task in the *Record Form*. The upper part of the box indicates the most relevant elemental functions within the section of the examination in which the task appears. For example, the Imitative Finger Movement task (*Record Form*, page 1) particularly involves the fine motor functions of somesthetic input and visual motor integration. The lower part of the box indicates other broad areas of function that may also have an impact on the performance of that task. In this case, attention, memory, and visual processing are other functions that are tapped on this task.

The tasks on the *PEEX 2* do *not* measure single elemental functions. There is no such thing as a task that requires only one function. Therefore, the clinician must recognize that there can be multiple reasons for failure on a particular task. The task analysis pages and the boxes indicating the most relevant elemental functions are provided to help the examiner make a clinical interpretation.

Normative Data

The original *PEEX* was for children between the ages of seven and nine. The *PEEX 2*, on the other hand, extends down to age six. By consulting the normative key to the left of each task on the *Record Form*, the examiner can conveniently assess whether or not the individual's performance on a given task is appropriate (generally within one standard deviation of the mean) for age. For example, on the Imitative Finger Movement task (*Record Form*, page 1), a six-year-old child would be expected to score between 4 and 7 correct responses. That is to say, the average range for this age group (±1 standard deviation from the mean) is 4 to 7. It can easily be seen that some tasks are clearly developmental while other tasks are not.

It is important that the examiner be aware of the need for *local norms*. It is likely, for example, that severely economically deprived children may perform on the *PEEX 2* in a manner that differs considerably from middle-class suburban children. Every effort has been made to eliminate serious cultural biases from the examination, but it is impossible to provide an absolutely culture-free assessment that taps multiple areas of ability. In particular, it is hard to separate language and culture. The examiner's awareness of this phenomenon can minimize its impact.

Components of the *PEEX 2*

The *Record Form* consists of five major sections that correspond to broad constructs of neuro-developmental function: fine motor/graphomotor, language, gross motor, memory, and visual processing. There are three checkpoints at which attention can be rated. This affords an opportunity to detect differences in strength of attention elicited by different kinds of tasks. Successive ratings also enable the examiner to document patterns of attention over time. Associated movements (AM) are indicated at particular points during the examination. These minor neurological indicators are often encountered in children with attention deficits and learning disorders. Finally, the child's use of strategies is rated on certain tasks. These ratings are included because it has been shown that children who use their own techniques to improve learning often have a positive outlook and may be more amenable to acquiring new techniques to enhance school performance. There is also a general health assessment page where a physician can summarize the results of a complete physical, neurological, and sensory examination. Finally, the examiner can record an overview of overall diagnostic findings on the summary impressions page. There is no specific scoring system for the summary impressions.

The *PEEX 2 Response Book* is used by the student in carrying out some of the tasks. The *Stimulus Book* contains pictures and other items relevant to certain tasks on the examination. This should not be written in or otherwise defaced, as it is to be used for repeated administrations of the *PEEX 2*. In addition to the three books, a sharp pencil, a stopwatch, and a squash ball are required. The *Observation Form*, an optional material, is designed to assist parents and others who observe the child's examination as well as to elicit information and comments from them that may be useful to the examiner.

Administration and Scoring

Before we discuss the specific tasks on the *PEEX 2*, some general points about administration are in order.

The first concerns the important issue of standardization in administration. Subtests have been organized in such a way as to give the children considerable variety and some physical breaks during the examination. The testing should occur in a quiet room in a comfortable atmosphere. The examiner should sit to the left or to the right of the child at a table; this may be less intimidating than sitting across the table from the child. The child may sometimes need reassurance and should be given encouragement and positive reinforcement throughout the examination.

In order to meet standards of reliability, it is important to administer the *PEEX 2* in a standardized way: the tasks should be given in the same order as they are listed and examiners should follow the instructions in this manual. Such a standardized administration is especially important when the instrument is applied for research or other group data base compilation.

These neurodevelopmental examinations have always been considered dynamic assessment tools with some flexibility of administration essential if the clinician is to use them to obtain the maximum amount of therapeutically useful information about strategies, modifications, and stylistic issues. Clearly, on some occasions clinicians must decide to modify a task, provide additional information, or make other allowances in order to explore the possible reasons for a student's difficulty. A clinician's alteration of a task in such a way as to allow a child to succeed, for example, by administering commands more slowly, may have major implications for teaching that child. When a given task is causing excessive frustration and providing no additional information, the examiner may decide not to complete it.

Throughout this manual scripts (indicated in quotation marks) are provided for instructing the child how to perform specific tasks. Such directions need not be used *verbatim*. Rather, they are meant to provide general guidelines for communicating what the child is expected to do. While it is important to include the entire content of each instruction, the examiner should feel free to do so in his or her own words.

It is helpful to have parents observe the administration of the *PEEX 2* unless there is concern that this might make a particular child too apprehensive. As observers, they may then become active participants in the evaluation process. Further, feedback from the clinician can be much more vivid and meaningful when the parents have observed directly the phenomena described by the examiner. Parents can also indicate to what extent the child's responses and behaviors during the examination were typical or atypical. The examiner can ask: ''Do you think this was typical? In general, do you think this was the way she usually performs?'' Parents' understanding of the *PEEX 2* can be enhanced by making use of the *Observation Form*, which explains each task and provides space for observers to record their direct observations and ideas about the child during the examination.

Although instructions for each task are not included in the *Record Form*, cues for the examiner facilitate recall of the administration and scoring. Those quantitative aspects of the scoring for which there are normative data are shaded, and the corresponding normative data are provided in boxes in the left-hand margins. Other more qualitative observations are scored on a 0,1 basis, with higher scores indicating normal or optimal performance. Certain items range from 0 to 2, and the criteria for determining the score are shown in a key. For example, the Attention Checkpoint scoring key provides specific criteria for rating a child's attention during specific parts of the examination. Items that can be summed to form a summary score (associated movements/synkinesia and strategies) are designated with an abbreviation in the right-hand margin (AM and STRATS, respectively). In all ratings on the *PEEX 2* (with the few exceptions indicated in this manual), a lower score represents poor performance while a higher score represents more proficient performance. Exceptions include items for which a specific amount of time to complete a task is recorded.

The behavioral observations page is unchanged from the original *PEEX*. It provides the examiner an opportunity to rate the student's responsiveness to the examiner, compliance with the examination, confidence, and rapport with the examiner. Also, the degree of performance anxiety, the range of affect, the stability of affect, and the spontaneity of communication can be noted.

The task analysis section of the *PEEX 2* is useful because all items measure *more than one* area or aspect of development. Divided into various cognitive and motor elements, it helps the examiner tease out specific developmental functions. For example, when a child copies a geometric form, both visual input and significant fine motor output are involved. Therefore, poor performance might reflect difficulty in either area of development or perhaps in both. In the task analysis section, the examiner indicates in all boxes across the form the child's developmental attainment level for each item. At the end of the examination, specific inputs and outputs can be totaled and specific deficiencies and strengths discerned.

In addition to the quantitative aspects of scoring, there are many opportunities for the examiner to make notations or record other comments about characteristics of the child's performance. These observations can also be instructive in the interpretation of overall performance.

The summary impressions page provides space for the examiner to record overall impressions and qualitative observations on a single page. This can be useful for report writing or for quick reference. There is no specific scoring system for this grid.

Recommendations

- The neurodevelopmental examination should never be performed in isolation. It is intended to be supplemented by educational testing and historical information gathered through interviews and/or questionnaires (such as *The ANSER System*). Such information should be obtained from parents, other clinicians, and from relevant school personnel.

- It is especially helpful to compare findings on the neurodevelopmental examination to other testing the child has had or is currently undergoing. One can thus seek "recurring themes" or patterns of findings that derive from multiple sources and thus validate or help modify one's interpretation of a child's profile of strengths and weaknesses and the reasons for particular difficulties.

- While normative data have been obtained for all of the items on the neurodevelopmental examinations, there can be local variation that may depend upon cultural, socioeconomic, and other variables. Therefore, it is most desirable to obtain local norms within the community where the examinations are to be given.

- The neurodevelopmental examinations do not generate a specific score or label. They are meant to contribute to a descriptive profile of strengths and weaknesses. Such a description is intended to yield an individualized management plan for the student.

- Validation studies of the neurodevelopmental examinations are currently underway. Users of the examination are encouraged to conduct such studies examining how specific findings on these assessments predict distinct forms of academic difficulty (such as delays in reading comprehension or problems with legibility in writing).

- Clinicians using the neurodevelopmental examinations should have proper training as well as sufficient practice in their use. Ideally, they should attend courses on neurodevelopmental function and variation. They should also observe and score a videotape* of the examination to determine their reliability.

- Those who use the examinations should be familiar with the conceptual framework and knowledge upon which they are based.**

*Available from Educators Publishing Service, Inc.
**EDITOR'S NOTE: Those who are unfamiliar with the concepts will find it helpful to read one or more of Dr. Mel Levine's books (see bibliography).

Specific Tasks

The following sections describe each item on the *PEEX 2*, including the rationale for its inclusion on the examination and specific guidelines for its administration, scoring, and interpretation.

Fine Motor/Graphomotor Functions

The fine motor and graphomotor tasks cover a wide range of components. Included are items entailing praxis, eye-hand coordination, motor speed, graphomotor speed, motor memory, somesthetic input, precise distal function, and motor sequencing. Several tasks requiring keen fine motor function are included on other portions of the examination. These include the Geometric Form Copying and Motor Sequential Imitation tasks in the Memory section. Throughout the Fine Motor/ Graphomotor Functions section, examiners are asked to make observations of synkinesias (mirror movements) and associated mouth movements. Synkinesias are frequently seen in children with attention deficits, while associated mouth movements are fairly common in children with fine motor dysfunctions, especially dyspraxias (motor planning problems).

Lateral Preference

Rationale: The Lateral Preference task is designed to determine a child's hand and eye preference. The literature on neurodevelopmental variation is inconclusive about the significance of left-handedness or preference for the left eye. However, there are some indications that poorly established dominance or mixed dominance (left-eyed and right-handed, for example) is commonly encountered among children with learning and/or attention problems. This task is also helpful in initiating the *PEEX 2* since it is not at all threatening or intimidating to children.

Administration: First the child is asked to demonstrate hand preference. She should be told: "First, make believe you are writing something on the table." The child then shows preference for one hand or the other while writing. Three other commands are given as follows: "Pretend you are throwing a ball over there." "Make believe you are hammering a nail into this table." "Now pretend you are brushing your teeth."

Scoring:
- 0 = Mixed preference
- 1 = Left hand or eye
- 2 = Right hand or eye

The scoring does not imply a numeric range of function, but is a categorical score.

Interpretation: There is no strong evidence for a greater number of learning problems among left-handed individuals. However, there are indications that children who show poorly established (that is, inconsistent) dominance may be at greater risk for these difficulties—perhaps because of a lack of complete hemispheric dominance in the brain. Further, students with mixed dominance have been found to have a higher than expected prevalence of school problems. Thus, findings of mixed or incomplete dominance can support other evidence in showing that a child may be neurologically predisposed to learning difficulty.

Imitative Finger Movement

Rationale: This test elicits evidence of finger agnosia (poor finger localization). It has been included on the *PEEX 2* because some children with writing problems have trouble localizing their fingers without close visual monitoring, which slows down their writing and makes the act tedious. Also, finger agnosia has been shown to coexist often with other forms of neurodevelopmental dysfunction. Visual registration and attention are also important components of this task as the child watches and imitates the examiner's finger movements. Finger agnosia is also one of the characteristics of the so-called Developmental Gerstmann Syndrome.

Administration: The *PEEX 2* tries to minimize effects of attention and memory. Therefore, when administering the Imitative Finger Movement task, the examiner should maintain the specific finger opposition until the child opposes his fingers. The child should be given the following instructions: "Now we are going to play a little game with our fingers. I would like you to put your hands up next to your head just the way I am doing it. I want you to keep your fingers back where you can't see them. I am going to move my fingers a certain way. Each time I move one of *my* fingers, I want *you* to move the *same finger* that I moved on my hand. I'm going to start with this hand (examiner's left) and you start with that hand (examiner points to the child's right hand). Here goes." (See Figure 1.) The examiner then proceeds to do each finger opposition as indicated on the *PEEX 2 Record Form.* Fingers are numbered as follows:

1 = thumb, 2 = index finger, 3 = middle finger, 4 = ring finger, 5 = little finger.

He should look for synkinesias on the contralateral hand and for hesitancy, false starts, and visual monitoring (cheating).

Scoring: Compute the total correct. The child performs four imitative finger movements with the right hand and four with the left hand, giving a total of eight.

Synkinesia, visual monitoring, and impulsivity:
   0 = Present
   1 = Absent
Hesitancy/false starts:
   0 = More than 2 times
   1 = Two times or fewer

Figure 1. For the Imitative Finger Movement task the examiner and child turn to face each other. The examiner moves her fingers individually; the child moves the same fingers on the hand that is the mirror image of the examiner's. The child's palms are held in the plane of his ears so that he may not look at his own fingers.

Associated movements, when present, are scored as a *0* on the *Record Form*; when absent, as a *1*. For each *0* next to Synkinesia or Associated Movement, the examiner should also circle the letters *AM* in the right-hand margin.

Interpretation: Poor performance is usually indicative of finger agnosia. Further supporting evidence can be sought during pencil and paper tasks, especially by watching the degree to which the child visually monitors pencil movement. Additionally, many children with finger agnosia develop a pencil grasp in which their thumbs wrap around their fingers, thereby immobilizing the distal joints of their fingers. They may do this because they have trouble knowing where those small joints are during writing. Sometimes they reveal other evidence of weakness in motor feedback such as problems with somesthetic input on gross motor tasks like Sidewise Tandem Gait and Sustained Motor Stance.

Finger Tapping

Rationale: This task enables the examiner to make determinations of a child's control over distal finger musculature. Some children show signs of dyskinesia or dysmetria on this activity. Such findings have been found to correlate with learning difficulties as well as dysfunctions of attention. Affected children may have difficulties sustaining a fine motor rhythm, which may ultimately affect the acquisition of keyboarding skills as well as other pursuits demanding rapid finger movements.

Administration: The examiner should demonstrate this procedure of tapping the index finger 20 times while the task is timed. She should put both hands on the table and begin with the dominant hand, showing the child that the index finger needs to rise from the table from one-half to one inch. The child should be told: "I would like you to tap like this 20 times, and I want to see how long it takes you. I will count your taps and use my timer. Remember now, only move the one finger. All of the other fingers on both hands should be down on the table." If the child moves the finger less than one-half inch from the surface, the examiner should stop the trial and remind the child to lift her finger higher. A second trial may be given with each hand if the child has obvious difficulty. The examiner then scores the better of the two trials. Observations of any associated mouth or finger movements should also be noted.

Scoring: The number of seconds for each trial is recorded and averaged for each hand in the shaded space. Other observations are recorded as *0* or *1*.

Associated movement, synkinesia, and dyskinesia/dysmetria:

0 = Present

1 = Absent

Interpretation: A child's finger tapping movements may be erratic and lacking in a smooth flow, or she may demonstrate what looks like "stickiness," a tendency for the fingers to adhere to the surface of the table or desk on which she is tapping. Such impaired performance on the task might be due to overall reduced motor speed or problems with the precise control of distal musculature. If this is the case, it may be helpful to look for evidence of slow output reflected in other tasks, which may be related to reduced rate of accomplishing school work. It is also helpful to examine distal movements during pencil and paper tasks, especially writing, where there is a need for rapid successive motor movements.

Many children with attention deficits appear to have difficulty suppressing movement with the contralateral fingers during tapping. Some individuals (especially those with motor production difficulties) are apt to display associated mouth movements.

Pencil Control

Rationale: This untimed task provides a measure of the precision with which a child can control a pencil. It offers observers a chance to evaluate pencil control in the absence of memory, language, and significant drainage of attention. Thus, a motor baseline can be derived for the evaluation of children with written output problems. The mazes have been designed to capture the most common and relevant forms of motor movement needed in letter formation. The task provides another opportunity to observe the child's pencil grip and the distance of eyes from the page, although these are not specifically recorded. The examiner can also observe whether the child is impulsive or works at a frenetic tempo. Does this child watch where he is going? Does he allow speed to take precedence over accuracy?

Administration: The child should be told: "We are now going to play a little game with a pencil. I would like you to put your pencil point down where it says *start* over here (the examiner points to the starting point of the first maze). When I tell you to start, I would like you to take your pencil and make believe it is a bicycle that you are riding along this funny road. You have to stay in between the lines with your pencil. Don't touch either line while you are drawing. I want to see if you can get all the way to the end, trying very hard not to touch either of these lines, staying in between them. Now you can start." After the child finishes, he should complete the second maze. "You do this one in the same way. Go from this dot to that dot."

Scoring: The examiner computes the total number of contacts (places the pencil line touches or crosses the printed line) with the lines on both mazes, and enters this number on the *Record Form*.

    Associated movement and impulsivity:
      0 = Present
      1 = Absent

Interpretation: Poor performance usually indicates difficulty with basic pencil control. It may suggest problems with eye-hand coordination. That is, the child may have difficulty programming a motor response that is based upon direct visual input. This could contribute to difficulty copying from a chalkboard or overhead transparency. Inattention to detail and impulsivity may also compromise performance. A child who does well on the untimed task but poorly when timed (see next task) may be revealing overall problems with the rate of output. This may also be reflected in other tasks on the *PEEX 2* and may suggest difficulties keeping pace with the demands for efficient output on paper and elsewhere in the curriculum.

Pencil Speed

Rationale: This task is somewhat similar to Pencil Control, except that it stresses speed. It is included to allow for comparisons of motor function under timed and untimed conditions. Rate is highly relevant since children must be able to move a pencil through letter forms fast enough to keep pace with the flow of their thoughts and the production of the language needed to express them.

Administration: The child is given the following instruction: "This is a little bit like what you just did, but this time I want to see how *fast* you can go. You should still try not to touch the lines, but you should work quickly to see how far you can go. Keep drawing your line until I say *stop*. . . . O.K., begin." The examiner records the total number of units that the child completes in 15 seconds.

Scoring: Total units are the number of units that are completed (the line must have passed the lower right-hand corner of the square wave). Total intersections are the number of contact points where the child's line touches or crosses over the printed line. Intersections are subtracted from units to derive the corrected total.

    Associated Movements:
      0 = Present
      1 = Absent

Interpretation: Inaccurate performance on this task may indicate poor pencil control or impulsivity. Sometimes, on the so-called speed-quality tradeoff, a child may opt to perform this task as quickly (and carelessly) as possible. Such a finding may indicate an overall impulsive/frenetic approach to work output. On the other hand, accurate movement produced at a slow rate suggests difficulty with motor speed, which could portend problems keeping up with the rate and synchrony demands that are critical for fluent and effective writing.

Write Alphabet

Rationale: The alphabet writing task involves multiple developmental functions. First, it affords an opportunity to observe handedness for writing. Second, it is a test of long-term motor memory for both letter gestalts and letter sequences. Third, it provides an opportunity to observe the child's pencil grasp and style of writing.

Administration: The child should use a well-sharpened pencil. Since alphabet writing is timed, the child should be told: "I want to see how much of the alphabet you can write in one minute. You don't have to write the whole alphabet, just as much as you can do in one minute. But don't rush; do a very good job." The child should not be instructed to do it as quickly as possible, but just "the way you normally do it." The child then writes the alphabet on page 1 of the *Response Book.*

Scoring:
Handedness:
0 = Left
1 = Right

The examiner records the number of letters legibly and correctly written in one minute, and 1 point is given for each letter (numbers are provided for every fifth letter to assist the examiner). Other qualitative observations such as the presence of reversals, quality of letter formations, or presence of associated movements, should be scored as indicated on the *Record Form.*

The criteria used for assigning points on the Graphomotor Observation Grid are shown on the grid itself. As usual, higher scores indicate normal performance. The completion of this observation grid is optional.

Interpretation: Letter reversals may indicate spatial confusion (poor directionality), impulsivity, or simply a memory overload during writing. Children with sequencing problems may have trouble recalling the order of movements needed to form letters. They may also have problems with the precise retrieval of the order of letters of the alphabet, sometimes having to go back to the start of the alphabet or to subvocalize an alphabet song. Some children with memory and/or attention problems will omit letters.

The examiner should be as specific as possible in describing a child's method of controlling the pencil. A loose, changing, or extremely tight grasp may suggest a graphomotor production deficit. A fistlike grip with overuse of proximal muscles and joints might imply weaknesses of propriokinesthetic feedback from the distal joints, that is, finger agnosia (see also the description of the Imitative Finger Movement task). Other observations can be equally revealing. Some children who have difficulty with pencil control and feedback tend to keep their eyes excessively close to the page. Such observations can be documented on the Graphomotor Observation Grid. Children whose performance on this task is slow for age are likely to have graphomotor dysfunctions and/or retrieval memory problems. For some older children whose letter formations are poorly automatized, the task requires considerable effort and leads to fatigue. It is not surprising that such children's output lags far behind their oral expression and ideation (developmental output failure).

The Graphomotor Observation Grid

This grid should be completed as a way of summarizing certain key findings in the motor domain that are likely to reflect writing facility. Observations of pencil grip, fluency, and other parameters are recorded during the alphabet writing task, or the examiner can use a separate piece of paper and ask a child to write a few sentences about a specific topic. The examiner should try to use the same topic for all children within an age group, so as to allow for comparisons. The grid can also be used to gauge a child's progress in writing over time.

Imitate Gestures

Rationale: This is a fine motor praxis task. In imitating gestures, a child must be able to mobilize the proper muscles to accomplish the activity based upon a visually presented model. Some children with dyspraxias have great difficulty imitating gestures.

Administration: The examiner says: "I want you to try to do what I do with my hands." The examiner demonstrates each of the four gestures shown in Figure 2. Each gesture should be formed out of the child's view. The child attempts to imitate each of these while the examiner maintains the configuration with his fingers. The quality of the imitation is recorded. In the case of the gestures requiring only the dominant hand, it is appropriate to look for synkinesia on the nondominant side of the child. The examiner should not provide any verbal cues during this task.

Scoring:
> 0 = Definite errors or inability to imitate gesture
> 1 = Correctly, but slowly or with difficulty
> 2 = Quickly and correctly

Interpretation: Poor performance may be evidence of dyspraxia. In particular, children with dyspraxia are likely to have trouble making use of visual-spatial information to program a fine-motor response. It may also be hard for them to develop a plan of action so that the right muscles can function in the right manner to create the hand pattern being shown to them. Other evidence for this might be seen in poor performance catching a ball (see page 27) or difficulty copying designs (see page 36).

Some children may have visual-spatial processing problems that affect their ability to mimic a visually presented static motor pattern or a dynamic action. Their motor function seems good but they have problems with the visual-spatial interpretive part of the task. They may perform well on tasks that do not have a strong visual-spatial input, such as motor tapping.

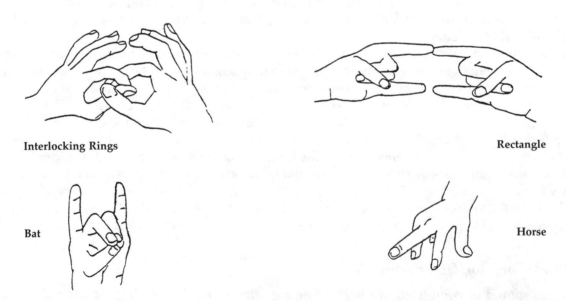

Interlocking Rings   Rectangle

Bat   Horse

Figure 2. The examiner demonstrates each of the four gestures, making them out of view of the child.

12

Attention Checkpoints

Rationale: During a neurodevelopmental assessment, patterns of concentration, motor activity, mental fatigue, and other parameters of attention can be readily observed using a wide range of tasks over an extended period. There are three such ratings of attention during the *PEEX 2*. Repeated observations allow the examiner to detect differences in behavior and attention that relate to changing demands of the examination or increasing fatigue as the examination proceeds. Giving a child developmentally appropriate challenges elicits certain patterns of attention that a clinician might not be able to observe while taking a history or performing a routine physical examination. Patterns of attention can be elusive to capture and inconsistent in their day-to-day or even moment-to-moment manifestations. Therefore, the extended observations facilitated on the *PEEX 2* can be revealing; they are especially germane when integrated with other information about the function or dysfunction of a child's attention.

Scoring: Ten parameters of attention are rated during the examination. These are described on the grid. The criteria for assigning scores is as shown in the key and as described more fully below.

    0 = Observed on more than one task
    1 = Observed on one task
    2 = Never observed

Although the scoring is open to different interpretations, which may compromise reliability, the descriptions shown in the checkpoint should be used to determine the score. In order to improve the reliability of these observations, it may be helpful for the examiner to make abbreviated notations in the *Record Form* when these signs of attention are observed, for example, IMP for impulsivity or FAT for fatigue. These can then be considered when assigning the score.

As with all of the *PEEX 2*, a higher score indicates a child with less of a problem. It is important to be aware, however, that a child's overall score on a section may not be nearly as important as the persistence of a particular trait. For example, a repeated observation that a child experiences tremendous mental fatigue during cognitive tasks is an important finding, one that will need to be noted and managed, even if other traits of dysfunctional attention are not so prominent. Finally, examiners need to be aware of the possibility that anxiety is creating attention difficulties for the child. Such anxiety can be documented later in the examination under Behavioral Observations.

1. *Impulsivity vs. Planfulness*—A child should be rated as impulsive if she proceeds with more than one task too quickly or if there is no evidence of planning or premeditation prior to engaging in it. In some cases, a child might begin a task before the examiner finishes the directions.

2. *Frenetic vs. Appropriate Tempo*—A child whose tempo is considered frenetic works much too quickly on a task and that rapid pace compromises the quality of performance. A child who works very fast and performs very well need not be rated as having frenetic tempo.

3. *Poor vs. Strong Attention to Detail*—A child shows poor attention to detail if he seems to get the overall gist of a task but misses some of the salient features.

4. *Distractibility vs. Resistance to Distraction*—Various forms of distractibility include a tendency to comment on sounds outside the room, to keep looking around, to ask "What's coming next?" or "When will this be over?" (distraction by the future), or to show evidence of free flight (distraction by association). Any of these signs exhibited during a task represent indicators of distractibility and should be so rated.

5. *Mental Fatigue vs. Resistance to Fatigue*—The child who yawns, stretches, or displays other gestures suggesting exhaustion or attempts to fend off such fatigue during the task should be rated as showing fatigability.

6. *Deterioration over Time vs. Sustained Quality*—Deterioration over time may include beginning a task well and then declining in the quality of performance as that task proceeds. It may also

include poorer performance on the tasks in a latter part of a section than on earlier tasks in that section.

7. *Inconsistent vs. Consistent Performance*—Inconsistent performance occurs when a child has made consecutive errors and then performs well on consecutive items. It might also be suspected when a child fails on easy items while succeeding on more challenging ones. In general, unpredictable or unaccountable patterns of error can often be taken as indications of performance inconsistency.

8. *Poor Self-Monitoring vs. Good Self-Monitoring*—A child with poor self-monitoring skills tends not to notice errors or constantly fails to look back over what has been done.

9. *Gross Overactivity vs. Large Motor Control*—An overactive child shows a pattern of having trouble sitting still, constantly changing body position, and/or getting up and walking around periodically.

10. *Fidgetiness vs. Small Motor Control*—A fidgety child exhibits considerable motion of the hands and/or feet. Repetitive tapping of the feet might be one example of such fidgetiness.

Interpretation: Some children display attention problems throughout the *PEEX 2*. However, a child may demonstrate difficulties with attention only at certain points, such as during the language section, which might suggest that she has predominantly weaknesses of auditory attention, or that her weaknesses of attention are secondary to problems processing and producing language. Of course, it should be borne in mind that the language section is probably the most demanding of attention to detail in general. Some children may gradually deteriorate in attention as the examination progresses. In this case attention ratings would be much lower at checkpoint three than at checkpoint two or one. Attention problems that are more prominent at the beginning of the examination may suggest the presence of performance anxiety.

These checkpoints are helpful, too, in determining which of the specific forms of dysfunctional attention are present in a particular child. Thus, some students may show considerable mental fatigue, while others may reveal mainly motor manifestations of attention difficulties or great difficulty with planning and self-monitoring. Such findings can then be compared to teacher and parent ratings of these particular parameters (for example, by using *The ANSER System Parent* and *School Questionnaires*). The identification of recurring patterns of this sort can then be used to derive a management plan to deal with the specific attention controls that are causing problems for the child.

The attention ratings have been found to correlate significantly with other independent measures of attention, but they (like all observations of attention) need to be interpreted with caution. Some children may appear attentive and engaged in the highly motivating setting and the one-to-one interaction provided by the neurodevelopmental examination session but evidence significant attention problems in school or at home. Such context-specific difficulties with attention are important to recognize; they, too, may have management implications.

Language Functions

The language section of the *PEEX 2* is intended to evaluate a wide range of functions relating to receptive and expressive linguistic competencies. Many of these items are critically important to the acquisition of reading skills. Others relate strongly to writing, to the processing of verbal explanations and instructions in the classroom, and to communication skills in general. The section begins with tasks assessing phonology and proceeds to single-word naming tasks using a variety of clues. Some of the subsequent tasks, which examine comprehension and expression at the sentence level, place high demands on memory and attention. The language section concludes with a task of passage comprehension.

Phonological Awareness

Part A—Rhyming

Rationale: Rhyming ability can be one indication of a child's sensitivity to phonemes (language sounds). Rhyming also requires a child to match phonemes to real words. As such, it tests the linkage between phonology and semantic abilities. There is also a significant memory component, as a child must search his "lexicon" and recall specific words within which are the sounds to be matched. These processes must be done at a rapid rate, since the rhyming task is timed. In the real world of school, such rapid access to phonological memory is a necessity.

Administration: The child is told: "Now we are going to play a rhyming game. I am going to tell you a word, and I would like you to tell me as many words as you can that rhyme with the word. Let's try a practice word. If I said the word *lick*, you could say *stick* or *tick*. Can you name some words that rhyme with *lick*?" The child then names a few such words. If the child makes a mistake, the examiner should correct her. Then the examiner says: "Now let's try another word. Can you make as many words as you can that rhyme with *hot*?" The task is repeated with the word *rake*. "Now let's see how many words you can say that rhyme with *rake*."

Scoring: The total correct in 20 seconds should be recorded. Only real words that truly rhyme should be counted.

Phonological errors should be recorded. These are either words or non-words that don't actually rhyme with the stimulus word.

The total number of non-words should also be recorded. These are word responses that either rhyme or do not rhyme with the stimulus word and are not actual words in English.

Part B—Phoneme Segmentation

Rationale: A considerable amount of research demonstrates a substantial correlation between children's ability to take apart sounds in words and put them together again and the effectiveness with which they develop decoding skills for reading and encoding skills for spelling. In the phoneme segmentation tasks, children are asked simply to listen to a word and tell the examiner how many sounds there are in that word. This, of course, requires the child to segment the word into its constituent phonemes. To do so, the child must have a keen awareness of the distinctiveness of individual phonemes within words.

Administration: The examiner should begin by saying: "We are now going to play a little game in which you have to listen carefully while I say some words. After I say each word, I would like you to tell me how many sounds there are in the word. For example, when I say the word *take*, there are three sounds." The examiner should then demonstrate the three sounds in the word *take*, using the series of circles on page 1 of the *Stimulus Book*. The examiner then says: "Now let's practice one. How many sounds are there in *luck*?" The child then tries to sound out *luck*. If he has difficulty with this, the examiner can demonstrate. Following this, the examiner says: "Now we are going to try some more words. How many sounds are there in . . . ?"

Scoring:
  0 = Incorrect
  1 = Correct
  The correct responses are shown in parentheses.

Part C—Substitution

Rationale: Substitution tasks represent another means of assessing phonological awareness. These particular kinds of exercises have been shown to correlate highly with overall reading performance in third and fourth grade. They are good predictors of the ability ultimately to automatize the sound system within words. Children who have difficulty with such phonological manipulations tend to be labored readers as they proceed through elementary school. They are apt to have problems decoding unfamiliar words.

Administration: In this task the child is told: "We are now going to try to change some words around. I am going to tell you a word. Then I am going to ask you to change the first sound in the word to a different sound, and I want you to tell me what the new word is. I'll give you an example: If you change the /m/ sound in *moose* to /g/, you get *goose*. How about if you change the /b/ in *bat* to /h/?" It is important for the examiner to pronounce the **sounds** of the letters, not the names. The examiner then proceeds to give the child the words on the list and to score each one that is correct. It is permissible to repeat an item. However, it is important to note each repetition. Such a need may be indicative of weaknesses of active working memory or attention.

Scoring:
    0 = Incorrect
    1 = Correct
The correct responses are shown in parentheses.

Interpretation: Reduced awareness of phonemes is commonly found in children who are experiencing problems acquiring skills in reading and spelling. Such students may have trouble processing (and, in some cases, producing) these sound units. It may therefore be difficult for them to associate sounds with letter symbols. Affected children often show problems manipulating and/or separating out the phonemes in words. Such problems may be revealed through poor performance on the segmentation and substitution tasks described above. Students with impaired performance on these activities are likely to have trouble decoding multisyllabic words. Their spelling may likewise reveal phonemic confusion (errors that are phonologically unpronounceable but visually close to the actual word). Some children with intact phonological processing may do poorly on rhyming because of gaps in retrieval memory. Others may have problems with the substitution task because they have limitations of active working memory (therefore being unable to hold the base word in mind while manipulating its sound content).

Picture Naming

Rationale: A number of research studies have shown a high correlation between rapid automatic naming skills and ability to decode written words rapidly. Picture Naming involves the associative linkage of a visual stimulus with a semantic and phonological entity (a word). A child's ability to name familiar objects quickly and accurately may reflect word retrieval skills as well as visual-verbal associative abilities. The Picture Naming task has been arranged to resemble the act of reading. Namely, the youngster is to go from left to right and name pictures just as if she were reading from left to right and naming the words.

Administration: The child is shown page 2 in the *Stimulus Book.* The examiner says: "You see all the pictures on this page? I would like you to go along from this side to this side on each line (the examiner points appropriately), and name each of these pictures just as quickly as you can. I want to find out how long it will take you to name all of the pictures on the page. Now you can begin."

This task is timed. The examiner should try to record exactly any incorrect responses to pictures. If a child cannot identify a picture, the examiner should write DK (don't know) next to the stimulus word on the *Record Form.* It is useful to differentiate between phonological errors and semantic errors. For example, if a child calls a dog a goose, that is a semantic error. If a child calls a duck a dock, that is a phonological error. If a child is unable to identify a picture at all, after *6 seconds* she should be told to skip it and go on to the next one. No prompts should be given during the administration of the task under timed conditions. After the administration of the entire task, the examiner has the option of assessing whether the child is more successful on missed items using phonemic cues (/thuh/ for item 6—thermometer) or semantic cues ("it stops you from getting rained on" for item 13—umbrella).

Scoring:

    0 = Incorrect

    1 = Correct

As indicated on the *Record Form*, the time in seconds, the total correct, the number of circumlocutions (substitutions of definitions or approximations of precise words) and hesitations (4 seconds or greater) should be recorded.

    Articulation:

    0 = Abnormal on more than one item

    1 = Normal

Interpretation: Poor performance on this task is usually related to weaknesses in word retrieval (automatized naming) and/or semantics (vocabulary). These deficiencies may be associated with a reduced sight vocabulary for reading, as a result of which word decoding is apt to be a slow and laborious process for a child. Sometimes children respond with words that sound similar to the correct response, representing imprecise phonological matching (*girang* for *giraffe*). Other errors suggest a pattern of imprecise semantic networking (*windsail* for *windmill*). Some children are poor at naming due to global problems with retrieval memory. They may ultimately have problems recalling math facts, spelling, and other precise data needed for school success, especially in the upper grades. The reasons for poor performance on picture naming may not be apparent until one examines other parameters of function (such as word retrieval with a verbal stimulus and other forms of retrieval memory). Rarely, children will struggle with this task because of severe problems with visual recognition.

Sentence Repetition

Rationale: Language ability at the sentence level may be the most revealing indicator of overall linguistic proficiency during the elementary school years. Sentence repetition assesses a child's ability to recall and reproduce sentences of increasing length and syntactic complexity. The appreciation of syntactic structures is crucial for the comprehension of oral and written language and can affect both academic performance and social communication. The recall of orally presented information is necessary for following directions and assimilating verbal explanations in the classroom. Sentence Repetition taps not only verbal memory but also the appreciation of semantics and syntax. If the words and the structure do not make sense to a child, he is likely to have great trouble repeating the sentence. Consequently, children with receptive language problems at the sentence level are likely to experience considerable difficulty on this task.

Administration: All children should be given all of these sentences. The examiner says: "I am going to read some sentences to you. I will read each sentence just once. After I have finished reading a sentence, you repeat it exactly the way I read it. Try to repeat every single word. Listen carefully because I can only read each sentence one time." The examiner then proceeds to read the sentences clearly and at a conversational rate. This task provides another opportunity for the examiner to screen articulation.

Scoring: Each sentence is scored.

    0 = Two or more errors or a significant distortion of meaning and/or syntax

    1 = One error with the overall syntax and meaning of the sentence preserved

    2 = No errors

    Articulation:

    0 = Abnormal on more than one word

    1 = Normal

Interpretation: Children with learning disorders may show evidence of morphological and/or syntactic difficulties on this task. In making morphological errors, they may change the verb tenses, and not use the conjunctions appropriately. Those with an underdeveloped appreciation of English grammar and sentence structure are likely to have particular problems repeating the complex sentences accurately. Others, who struggle with short-term memory but have strong language processing, may preserve the overall meaning but restate the sentences in their own words. Chunk size issues (the ability to process lengthy material) are important on this task, and attention problems occasionally compromise performance, as seen in the omission of articles or the alteration of tenses to yield sentences that still make sense and are grammatically correct.

Complex Sentences

Rationale: The Complex Sentences task is designed to elicit difficulties with comprehension of sentences. These sentences, each of which contains a discrete challenge, tap recent acquisitions in the development of language in six- to nine-year-old children. Such recent language milestones include the use of various types of embedded clauses, the understanding of conjunctions, the appreciation of temporal relationships, and the processing of passive forms. Table 1 summarizes the specific receptive language elements that are tapped by each of these sentences.

Administration: The child should be told: "I am now going to read you some sentences. After each sentence I will stop and ask you a question about the sentence to find out if you understood

TABLE 1

LANGUAGE CHALLENGES PRESENTED IN THE COMPLEX SENTENCES

Sentence	Language Challenge
1. The car is parked next to the garage.	A prepositional phrase (*next to*) that denotes location
2. Before the door was opened, the boy put his coat on.	The understanding of temporal prepositions (*before*); violation of order of mention (i.e., events do not occur in the order in which they are stated in the sentence).
3. The boy who liked the girl ran away down the street.	Violation of the minimal distance principle (i.e., the girl did not run away even though *girl* is closest to the verb); noun doing "double duty" as a subject of the independent and of the embedded dependent clause
4. The lion that the tiger bit jumped over the giraffe.	Sentence in which a noun has two functions: as the subject of the independent clause and as the object of the embedded dependent clause
5. The horse jumped over the fence after it started raining.	Same as sentence 2
6. The girl saw the man who was wearing green shoes.	Sentence in which a noun (*man*) is the object of the independent clause and the subject of the nonembedded dependent clause; obeys minimal distance principle
7. The clown who called the little dog ran into the tent.	Same as sentence 3
8. The car that was hit by the truck was driven by the man.	Passive form; a noun (*car*) is the object of the embedded dependent clause and also the passive subject of the independent clause; also somewhat contradicts expectations (of man driving truck), and therefore susceptible to impulsive responses

it. I can only say each sentence once, so you need to listen very carefully. Here goes." The examiner then reads each sentence and asks the questions about it. The correct responses are shown in the *Record Form.*

Scoring:

    0 = Incorrect

    1 = Correct

Interpretation: Children with language difficulties may not have yet attained the levels of proficiency and sophistication required for this task. Errors caused by weak verbal attention and/or fluctuating auditory registration in short-term memory may interfere with successful completion of this task. However, these sentences are concise, so that they do not require much verbal memory or sustained focus. The responses to each question are intentionally brief to enable the examiner to assess receptive language without the child's having to engage in much language production, which should be evaluated separately.

Verbal Instructions

Rationale: The Verbal Instructions task evaluates verbal comprehension, verbal memory, and attention to verbal detail. Many youngsters with language difficulties or attention deficits have trouble completing this task. In general, the items in the Verbal Instructions task are not as syntactically complex as those in the Complex Sentences task. However, they entail much more integration of memory and attention to fine detail with language. A component of this task involves the use of a verbal input to create a motor response.

Administration: The child is shown page 2 in the *Response Book.* She is told: "I want to find out how well you follow directions. You see the page in this book. If you look closely, you will notice that it has a whole bunch of things on it. At the top there are dots (the examiner points). There are five dots, two dots, three dots, four dots, and one dot. On the next line are three squares: A big square, a middle-sized square, and a small square. Then you see a bunch of Xs: a big X, a middle-sized X, and two small Xs. At the bottom there are circles: two big circles and two small circles. Now I am going to give you some directions. I am going to tell you things that I would like you to do on this page. Here is your pencil. Let's get started. Listen very carefully because I am not supposed to repeat any of these directions."

The examiner then gives the directions and scores according to whether or not the child is able to carry out the command accurately. It is useful to record any specific mistakes right on the *Record Form.* For example, if, when told to "touch the middle square with your pencil and then with your finger," the child touches the large square instead of the middle square, cross out the word *middle* on the form and substitute the word *large.* This makes it possible to go back and reread or recreate patterns in the child's errors, which may be very revealing. The instructions should be read at a conversational rate with normal phrasing and inflection. If a child is clearly struggling with the task, the examiner can make a number of accommodations to determine whether such strategies are useful. Items that were missed can be repeated, sometimes with a slower rate, chunking, or other accommodations. Alternatively, the student can be asked to repeat the instruction out loud.

Scoring:

    0 = Incorrect

    1 = Correct

Even minor errors of detail should be scored 0 (for example, if the child touches with her finger instead of with the pencil). Specific errors can be noted in the text of the instructions in the *Record Form.*

Interpretation: The Verbal Instructions task measures more than anything else a child's ability to handle relatively large chunks of language input. Thus, there is a significant memory component to this task, for it frequently requires the child to complete one part of the task while remembering and then subsequently accomplishing another aspect. In this way, active working memory for language is stressed. The pattern of responses can be particularly helpful in sorting out the relative contributions of sentence comprehension, attention, auditory registration in short-term memory, and active working memory. Active working memory deficits are frequently accompanied by difficulties in writing and math computation. Evidence for difficulties in these areas, as well as poor performance on other *PEEX 2* tasks involving active working memory, should be sought.

The first two items and the last two are identical, which is meant to help detect students who have problems with sustained attention and may therefore reveal discrepant performance over time. Children who show significant gaps on this task are at risk for serious problems in processing verbal directions and explanations in school. They may also experience difficulty dealing with the extended language content of text books. It should be noted that the ease or difficulty with which a child follows directions throughout the administration of the *PEEX 2* can also be used to evaluate receptive language function. If the examiner constantly feels the need to slow down, repeat, and/ or demonstrate, the student may be manifesting problems with language comprehension.

Sentence Formulation

Rationale: This task provides a useful assessment of expressive language fluency. Sentence formulation demands good verbal planning skills, an appreciation of English syntax, and some knowledge of morphology and semantics. The words to be used to form sentences become increasingly demanding. The child must form sentences that are grammatically correct. This task (along with Picture Naming, Rhyming, and Paragraph Summarization) provides insight into a child's expressive language abilities.

Administration: The child should be shown each word as it appears in the *Stimulus Book*. If the child is unable to read each word, the examiner should read the word to him. Otherwise, ask him to read the word. If the child hesitates or misreads the word, it is appropriate to offer a correction. Each stimulus word must be used exactly as presented. The child is not permitted to change plurality, tense, or any word endings. If he does so, it is permissible to correct him, pointing out, for instance, "The word is *made* not *make*."

The examiner states the following: "This is the word *car*. I am going to make a sentence with the word *car*: I see a car. Now, I am going to show you some other words, and I want to see if you can make up a sentence using each word. You may use any other words you want and make up any sentence you want. But you have to use the word exactly as it is. For example, if the word is *jump*, you cannot change it to *jumped*. Try to make a complete sentence. And, the sentence should make good sense. This is the word. . . . Now make a sentence that uses the word. . . ." If the child is unable to compose a sentence, the examiner should demonstrate: "I am reading a *book*." The child gets no credit and is asked to try the second item: "Let's go on and try to make another sentence now." When there are two words (*water, who*), the child should be told: "Now make up a sentence that has both of these words in it. You can use either one first."

Scoring: Apply the following criteria to each formulated sentence. 0 = No; 1 = Yes

Used all words—All words used in their proper tenses

Grammar—Sentence is grammatically correct

Complete sentence—Sentence is complete, not a phrase and not a run-on with many clauses

Meaningful—Sentence makes ordinary sense. (Bizarre or meaningless sentences should be scored 0.)

A maximum score of 4 is possible for each sentence. Record a total score where indicated on the *Record Form*.

Impulsivity:

0 = Impulsive (often seen when a child starts a sentence without thinking about fitting in the stimulus word)

1 = Appropriate

Ease of production:

    0 = Considerable hesitancy, more than one false start, or excessive effort

    1 = Some hesitancy or one false start

    2 = Notably quick and effortless formulation, without hesitancy

Interpretation: Sentence formulation difficulties are common among children with a range of learning disorders. Children with language production difficulties may reveal significant problems creating grammatically correct meaningful sentences. Or they may do so too slowly and with excessive effort required. Such labored performance may correlate with expressive language dysfluency and place a child at risk for trouble with both oral and written expression. Some children with adequate language abilities but poor planning and organizational abilities create disorganized run-on sentences or they may make multiple false starts rather than stopping and thinking ahead before producing the sentence orally. On the other hand, children with unusual verbal strengths or impressive creative abilities may produce especially interesting, imaginative, or complex sentences. Examiners may wish to record such sentences as evidence of cognitive strengths.

Paragraph Summarization and Comprehension

Rationale: This task provides some indication of a child's ability to process discourse, language that extends beyond the boundaries of sentences. Moreover, effective summarization and comprehension go well beyond basic processing. This task also involves expressive fluency (for summarization), various aspects of memory (including short-term registration, sequencing, and active working memory), and attention to detail. As children proceed into the upper elementary school grades, they must be prepared to process and assimilate increasingly large amounts of language orally and during reading. Not only do they need to understand such material but they must also be able to extract its most salient features for storage in memory. This section of the *PEEX 2* provides some indication of the ability to perform in this manner. Two separate passages are presented. The first of the paragraphs (A) is highly experiential and in narrative form. It is appropriate for younger children (ages 6 and 7) because this is the kind of discourse with which they are most likely to be familiar and experienced. Paragraph B, used for 8-year-olds, is expository and decontextualized. It is more typical of the kinds of comprehension demands that are placed on older elementary school students, requiring an ability to deal with information that is removed from direct experience.

Administration: The examiner says to the child: "Now I am going to read something to you. I am going to read a paragraph, and I would like you to listen to it very carefully. As soon as I am finished reading it, I would like you to summarize it—to say it back to me. I want to see how much of it you can remember and tell me." The examiner then reads the paragraph, following which the child is asked to summarize it. The passages should be read with plenty of inflection in order to make the stories particularly interesting. After the child has summarized the paragraph, the examiner immediately asks the six questions related to comprehension and the recall of specific details. Ordinarily, only one of these passages is given to a child. However, if an older child does poorly on passage B, the examiner might want to try passage A. Alternatively, a younger child who succeeds easily on passage A might then be challenged with passage B.

Scoring: The summarization is scored according to how many of the key facts (as noted on the *Record Form*) are included by the child.

    0 = Not mentioned or incorrect

    1 = Correct

The examiner also rates the child's preservation of the serial order of the material. In Passage A, item 3 of the summarization allows some flexibility, so that the child gets credit for saying either that Mary went to the store or that she bought some ice cream. In Passage B, several items of the summarization have specific criteria shown in the *Record Form*; for example, the child gets credit on item 5 for stating one or more of the three details.

Interpretation: To interpret difficulties with Paragraph Summarization and Comprehension, the examiner should look at findings from other parts of the *PEEX 2*, additional testing, and the child's history. The task requires the processing of large chunks of verbal information, so that children must retain details from the beginning of the paragraph as they proceed through it. Memory functions are therefore very important on this task. In addition, children need to sustain attention throughout the paragraph. Some children have difficulties with their summarization skills but, nevertheless, comprehend and can recall important details from a paragraph. They are more likely to succeed on the comprehension and recall section of this exercise while having difficulty with the summarization demands. These individuals may be manifesting difficulty with expressive language, sequential organization, saliency determination, or planning. Children with receptive language problems are more apt to have difficulty with both summarization and comprehension. They may miss or misunderstand the essential points of the passages. The stories are of considerable length, as a result of which children with attention deficits may be unable to sustain listening. They may miss critical details or substitute extraneous data from their own experience. Many students with weaknesses of active working memory tend to recall the end of the passage but retain little or no information from its beginning.

Gross Motor Functions

The gross motor section of the *PEEX 2* is very similar in its content to the gross motor section of the original *PEEX*. Problems with body position, balance, eye–upper limb coordination, and motor sequential abilities can be documented. Children who exhibit gross motor dysfunction may be at a distinct disadvantage socially, and they may also be at risk for a poor self-image. In particular, the combination of gross motor problems with academic delays is likely to have a serious negative impact on self-esteem. The detection of specific strengths in the gross motor realm, on the other hand, can be especially helpful in programming successful experiences, especially in the cases of students with learning difficulties.

Sustained Motor Stance

Rationale: This task is designed to examine vestibular function, somesthetic input, and body position sense. It is not unusual for a child to sway or temporarily lose balance during the motor stance. Children with good somesthetic feedback are able to self-correct without actually falling. Competency in athletic pursuits that demand good balance and body position sense (such as skiing and gymnastics) may be predicted in part during this activity. The task also enables the examiner to observe for signs of motor impersistence as well as choreiform twitches (involuntary rotary movements) of the outstretched tongue or fingers.

Administration: For this task the child is told: "Now I want you to stand up and put your feet close together. Put your arms way out in front of you, spread your fingers way apart, close your eyes, open your mouth, and stick your tongue *all the way* out (Figure 3A). That's fine. Now I want to see how long you can stay like that, as still as you can be." The examiner should correct any errors in the child's stance. The youngster is permitted one false start. That is to say, if the stance is not maintained for very long, there can be a second trial—the one that is actually scored. The examiner should not demonstrate. Maintaining the posture for less than 15 seconds or difficulty keeping the tongue or the fingers stretched out properly is considered impersistence (Figure 3B) and should be so noted. Observations of choreiform twitches and spooning of the fingers should also be made.

Figure 3A. This girl is executing the Sustained Motor Stance task optimally. Note that her hands are stretched out in front of her with her fingers spread wide apart, her tongue is protruding, and her eyes are closed.

Figure 3B. This girl shows evidence of motor impersistence. Her arms have descended, and her tongue has been withdrawn.

Scoring:
 Motor persistence:
  0 = Tongue darts in and out and/or arms descend more than 15 degrees or complete loss of stance or eyes open more than once
  1 = Tongue does not go in and out or eyes open more than once; arms do not drift downward more than 15 degrees
 Spooning:
  0 = Dorsal concavity (spooning) of fingers
  1 = No hyperextension of fingers
 Choreiform twitches (of tongue or fingers):
  0 = Circular rotary movements (not tremors) of outstretched fingers and/or tongue
  1 = No rotary movements

Interpretation: Motor impersistence is a common finding among children with attention deficits and hyperactivity, for whom motor inhibition is especially a problem. Children with poor somesthetic input and/or vestibular function may sway excessively and have difficulty maintaining the posture or self-correcting for their sways. Choreiform twitches in the tongue or the fingers have been well described in association with developmental and behavioral problems in school children. Spooning results from excessive tone in the extensor musculature and tendons of the hands that produces a concave appearance of the dorsum of the outstretched fingers. Impersistence, choreiform twitches, and spooning may all be indicators of minor neurological dysfunction.

Rapid Alternating Movement

Rationale: This task involves upper limb muscular coordination and includes motor planning, somesthetic input, sequencing, and motor facilitation and inhibition. It also entails the establishment and maintenance of a motor rhythm. A child should be able to inhibit proximal musculature (muscles of the shoulder girdle) while facilitating rapid motor movements in and around the distal musculature (forearm). An ability to do so results in flailing of the arm, a minor neurological indicator called dysdiadochokinesis. This task also permits the observation of associated hand or mouth movements.

Administration: The examiner should demonstrate the Rapid Alternating Movement task and ask the child: "Do you see how I am moving my hand? It is like opening and closing a doorknob. Can you keep your arm close to your body and do this the way I do it?" The examiner then stops doing the task, and the child tries it (Figure 4A). It should be done first on the dominant side and then on the non-dominant side. "Now do the same thing with your other arm." The task should be continued on each side for 10 seconds.

Scoring: The quality of the child's performance (dominant side and non-dominant side) should be noted as *1* or *0*.

  0 = Awkward, poorly sustained movement and/or obvious shoulder movement
  1 = Smooth movement without involvement of shoulder muscles

Proximal inhibition, synkinesia in the opposite hand, and associated movements of the mouth:

  0 = Present
  1 = Absent

Figure 4A. This boy is performing the Rapid Alternating Movement task well. His elbow is close to his trunk, while the muscles of his forearm are implementing the rapid alternating movement. In the meantime, the contralateral arm shows no associated movements. Nor are there any extraneous mouth movements.

Figure 4B. This youngster shows dysdiadochokinesis (poor inhibition of proximal muscle groups). This would be scored as a 0.

24

Interpretation: Children who exhibit dysdiadochokinesis may have trouble with the inhibition of proximal muscle groups while facilitating planned movements of more distal muscle groups (Figure 4B). Consequently, they are apt to exhibit excessive flailing or shoulder movement during this task. Poor performance on this task is often taken as evidence of neuromaturational delay. However, it may also be indicative of deficient motor control. Some children with attention deficits will manifest this finding as part of a much broader picture of weak facilitation and inhibition. Not only do they have trouble "deciding" which muscle groups to facilitate and which to inhibit, but they may also have parallel difficulties deciding which behavioral or cognitive actions to engage in and which to inhibit. The presence of synkinesia and other associated movements on this task contributes to the overall Associated Movements score (*Record Form*, page 10). As noted, the presence of multiple associated movements during the *PEEX 2* correlates with attention deficits and with certain forms of motor dysfunction.

Hopping in Place

Rationale: This task is included as an assessment of gross motor sequential planning and organization and of the ability to form and sustain complex motor rhythms. As with the previous task, both motor facilitation and motor inhibition are essential; the child must inhibit a third hop on each leg. The child also needs good body position sense and balance, although on this task visual feedback augments body position sense. The ability to form and sustain the pattern in sequential hopping is analogous to numerous common gross motor pursuits such as dribbling a basketball, jumping rope, or dancing.

Administration: The examiner provides the following instruction: "I would like to see how you do with hopping. I want you to hop two times on this foot and then two times on that foot and then again two times on this foot. Keep doing that until I tell you to stop. I don't want you to go any place. Do your hopping all in one spot. Are you ready? O.K. Let's go." The hopping is continued for 10 seconds.

Scoring:
> 0 = Unable to complete the hopping for even one cycle
> 1 = Some cycles are performed adequately and others inadequately
> 2 = Consistently good motor rhythmic production
> Dystonic posturing:
> 0 = Present
> 1 = Absent

Interpretation: Children who have difficulty with motor inhibition may tend to insert a third hop. Children with motor planning and/or motor sequencing problems find it difficult to develop the pattern smoothly. They keep hesitating between hops and thereby exhibit a lack of rhythmicity. Some individuals have trouble (or require repetition) translating the verbal instructions into a motor response; they may have also displayed such shortcomings during the Verbal Instructions task. Finally, a child sometimes does poorly because of an inability to maintain balance during hopping; generally weak self-monitoring or specific problems with body position sense may account for this.

Sidewise Tandem Gait

Rationale: This task requires that a child be adept at imitating a gross motor action. It is also an assessment of the ability to activate appropriate musculature in the lower limbs without engendering dystonic posturing. The Sidewise Tandem Gait involves body position sense, balance, and an ability to maintain a highly complex gross motor pattern. The child has to maintain that pattern while navigating toward a goal. Thus, a certain amount of previewing and self-monitoring is needed for successful completion of the task.

Administration: The child is told: "I would like you to watch me now. I am going to walk sidewise. Watch how I do it." The examiner then puts both feet together and moves her left foot around to the lateral side of the right foot. The two shoes should be touching each other (Figure 5). The examiner continues to walk this way. The child is then told: "Now I want you to try to walk sidewise. Stand up and face that wall. See if you can walk sidewise to here (a point ten feet from the starting point). The examiner watches for difficulty completing the task, errant pathways, and evidence of dystonic posturing. If a child has difficulty performing the task the first time, it is permissible for the examiner to provide a second demonstration. If the child is unable to perform the gait at all, the examiner may stop the attempt.

Scoring:
   0 = Unable to comply and imitate the gait
   1 = Performs well but in the wrong direction or inconsistently
   2 = Straight line performed well
 Dyskinesia and dystonic posturing:
   0 = Present
   1 = Absent

Interpretation: There are multiple reasons for difficulty with this activity. Children with poor balance (diminished body position sense and poor self-correction) may sway excessively and fall over. Those with motor planning problems and/or visual spatial confusion may have great difficulty imitating the gait. Others with deficient self-monitoring may go off course and pursue an erratic

A   **B**   **C**

Figure 5. The illustrations above depict a child completing the Sidewise Tandem Gait. Her hands are at her sides, and there are no indications of any dystonic posturing. Initially, she crosses her left leg in front of her right leg (A), placing the lateral aspect of her left foot against the lateral aspect of her right foot (B). She then brings the right foot behind the left leg (C) and places the medial aspects of her feet next to each other to complete one cycle of the Sidewise Tandem Gait.

Figure 6. The anteverted hand of this child while completing a Sidewise Tandem Gait should be noted. This represents a form of neuromaturational inefficiency or immaturity. If asymmetrical, it may suggest lateralized neurological involvement.

path. Those with minor neurological dysfunctions may show excessive dystonic posturing (extroversion of the arms) or anteversion of the hands (Figure 6) during the Sidewise Tandem Gait.

Catch Ball

Rationale: This task is a measure of eye–upper limb coordination. A child must judge a trajectory in space and predict its time and place of arrival. Rapid motor activation in the hands is then required to catch the ball. Success therefore entails a sense of "outer space" and accurate timing of the motor response. This form of activity plays a significant role in many sports, including football, baseball, and tennis.

Administration: The examiner stands 10 feet from the child. The child is told: "Do you see this little ball? I am going to throw it to you, and I would like you to catch it with *both of your hands.*" The examiner then throws the child the ball for two practice trials. The ball (a squash ball) should be thrown gently, aiming for the child's sternum.

Scoring: Record the total number of successful catches (out of six).

Interpretation: Some children are generally well coordinated but have problems interpreting the visual-spatial input (trajectory of the ball in space). They may have good body position sense and be able to run and swim fast, yet are inept at ball sports. Others, who may or may not have other evidence of motor difficulty, lack the planning functions and eye-hand coordination necessary to accomplish the task. It is helpful to note the consistency and accuracy with which the child returns the ball to the examiner. Many children with attention deficits appear to use a totally different throwing style each time they toss the ball back.

Total Associated Movements and Synkinesia Score

Scoring: All the items indicated as AM on pages 2 and 10 of the *Record Form* are added to form a total score at the bottom of page 10. Higher points on this scale are more optimal. Generally, children with associated movements noted on six or more occasions (total score of less than 13) are considered to show prominent signs of neuromaturational delay.

Memory Functions

The memory section of the *PEEX 2* surveys multiple parameters of mnemonic function. These include word memory, visual and auditory sequential memory, revisualization (visual retrieval), motor sequential recall, and convergent long-term retrieval. There is a mix of short- and long-term memory activities as well as variation in the modality of input. It is important to recognize that memory can never be evaluated as an independent function as it is always highly interactive with attention, with strategy use, with the quality and depth of processing, and with the presence or absence of anxiety. Therefore, deficient performance on any particular memory subtest may reflect weaknesses in these domains that interact with memory. In addition to the memory tasks contained on this section of the *PEEX 2*, some memory-laden items are contained in other sections. The Verbal Instructions task is one such example. To make a clear diagnosis of a memory disorder, it is helpful to integrate memory findings from the *PEEX 2* with direct samples of a child's academic work. In this way, a pattern of one or another form of memory dysfunction may emerge as a recurring theme.

Digit Spans

Rationale: The digit span is one of the most commonly used of all cognitive tasks because it measures a multitude of functions, including attention, freedom from anxiety, sequencing, the ability to deal with large chunks of data, the rate of processing, the use of mnemonic strategies, and short-term memory in general. Thus, it can be particularly helpful to see how poor performance on a digit span fits with other information about the child. There may be important hints about specific forms of processing or memory weakness.

Administration: The examiner says to the child: "Now I am going to tell you some numbers. I will say the numbers one at a time and when I am all finished, I would like you to say all of the numbers back to me in the same exact order that I said them to you." The examiner then says the numbers to the child as listed on the *Record Form*. The numbers should be articulated at a rate of one per second. There should be as little intonation as possible. The examiner should try to pronounce each number with the same degree of stress or emphasis. Every effort should be made to avoid extra emphasis or falling intonation on the last digit in a sequence. If the child does two of the four-digit spans correctly, the examiner proceeds to the five-digit spans. If two are not done correctly, the three-digit spans are administered. If the first two spans at any level are both correct or both incorrect, the child is not presented the third. Otherwise, all three should be given. In addition to recording whether the spans are repeated correctly or incorrectly, the examiner watches for the use of strategies in the form of subvocalization. The examiner should note whether or not the child uses any strategy (particularly subvocalization). It is also permissible to ask how the child did this task.

Scoring: The final score is the length of span at which the child is correct on two out of three items.

    0 = Incorrect
    1 = Correct
   Use of strategies:
    0 = None
    1 = Present; appears to whisper numbers or say them softly

Interpretation: Poor performance on the Digit Spans task may stem from a range of possible dysfunctions. Deficiencies of auditory registration, short-term memory in general, and sequential memory are the most prevalent possibilities. Attention deficits are also known to adversely affect performance of this task. Inconsistencies of attention may be suspected when a child displays a seemingly random error pattern (missing a shorter span and succeeding on a longer one). Some children are slow processors and cannot keep pace with the one-per-second recitation of the numbers. Others may have difficulty with number processing; they might be more effective with a word span or with the recall of a chain of letters instead of numbers. Thus, performance on the digit span can be impossible to interpret without knowing more about the child's patterns of functioning on other parts of the *PEEX 2* and elsewhere.

It is useful to observe the child's use of strategies on the Digit Spans. Subvocalization represents a rehearsal strategy that enables the child to recycle the input, creating firmer registration in short-term memory. Some children may form visual images of the numbers as the examiner presents them. As metacognition develops, children are able to articulate these strategies to others, and this capacity can also be assessed on this task.

Drawing from Memory

Rationale: This visual retrieval task is included because it is a reliable assessment of the registration in short-term memory of visual gestalt and detail. Thus, a child's ability to process relevant visually-presented stimuli and appreciate spatial relationships is an important part of drawing from memory.

The child must also be able to store such information for a short period. Attention, too, is a major component in this activity: a child must focus long enough and hard enough to retain the images. *Administration:* The child is told: "Now I am going to show you a whole bunch of designs. I would like you to study each of these pictures for 10 seconds if you need to. Then I will hide the picture and show you a picture that looks like the one that you studied but has something missing. You will have to fill in what's missing to make the second picture look just like the first picture. Now I will show you one of these designs. Look at it very carefully and try to remember everything about it." The child spends up to 10 seconds studying the first image (*Stimulus Book*, page 5). The examiner hides the page and the child is shown the corresponding design in the *Response Book* and asked to complete that design. The examiner should not go back and show the child the original design. For the last item (5), the child should be warned that you are going to give her an empty page, and that she will need to draw as much of the picture as she can remember.
Scoring:
    0 = Incorrect
    1 = Correct

Criteria for scoring are shown in the *Record Form*. The examiner should record the scores at the completion of the task. The total score is the sum of the individual items. In addition to recording the total score in the shaded area, the examiner can record how many of the five drawings were completed correctly or almost correctly by the child. For example, if the child gets four of the figures correct or almost correct, while getting one figure completely wrong, this should be recorded as 4.

Use of strategies such as rehearsal, imaging, or verbal mediation:
    0 = Absent
    1 = Present

Interpretation: Poor performance on this task may indicate generalized weaknesses in short-term memory or modality specific problems with visual registration. Alternatively, a child may have problems processing the actual visual designs. Some children with inconsistent attention find it hard to allocate sufficient attention to some or all of the figures. This is often reflected as inconsistent performance across the five figures. For example, a child with attention deficits may get three figures completely correct and two completely incorrect. Also, some children tend to do better on those figures that consist of sequences of simple figures or alphabetic/numeric symbols, whereas others do better on those figures that have to be processed as a visual gestalt. Such findings may be indicative of a preferred learning style (for example, for sequences or configurations).

Copying from memory can also be a good way to make observations of strategies, as some children facilitate memory function by describing the figures to themselves, sometimes barely audibly. Other children keep opening and closing their eyes while studying the forms, as if they are testing themselves. Such excellent strategic approaches represent definite strengths in a child within the *PEEX 2* age range. The motor aspects of this task are not challenging for this age group; therefore, it is unlikely that motor problems would account for weak performance unless such handicaps are very severe (as in the case of serious involuntary movements, such as tics).

Days of the Week

Rationale: The Days of the Week task represents an effort to elicit a child's mastery of practical sequences. The alphabet writing task does this as well. Reciting the days of the week requires long-term sequential memory and (in the case of saying them backward) active working memory. The rapid automatic naming of days is an indication that time and sequence are not excessively difficult for a child to appreciate and assimilate.
Administration: Children who are not yet eight should state the days of the week forward. Children who have reached their eighth birthdays should state them in reverse. If a child not yet age eight can state the days forward perfectly, ask him to try them backwards.

Scoring:
    0 = Errors
    1 = All correct

Interpretation: Difficulty on this task may indicate generalized problems with temporal-sequential organization and sequential memory. Children with sequencing problems are commonly delayed in learning the days of the week and the months of the year. They may also have a weakened sense of how time works. Recalling the days of the week (forward or in reverse) may be extremely time consuming and effortful for them. Retrieval of factual data from long-term memory stores may also be an important component of this task. For some children, therefore, impaired performance may constitute one indicator of generalized problems with convergent recall.

Word Learning

Rationale: The Word Learning task affords an opportunity to find out what it is like to teach the child using a verbal (semantic) input. Performance on this task requires strength of attention as well as memory, and is helped appreciably through the use of mnemonic strategies. Children with a strong sense of word meanings and so-called well-developed semantic networks may excel at word learning.

Administration: The examiner says to the child: "I am going to tell you some words, and I want you to try to remember all of the words. You can remember them in any order you want. You do not have to say them back in the same order that I said them to you. I just want to find out how many of them you remember. Now, here goes." The examiner says each word clearly with no intonation at a rate of one per second. The child is then told: "Now, let's see how many of those words you can say back to me." The examiner indicates on the *Record Form* which words were recalled. If the child does not recall all of the words on the first trial (a strong likelihood), the examiner says: "Now I am going to say the same words to you again. Then I will find out how many you can remember all over again." The same procedure is used to record the second trial. A maximum of four trials should be used. Once the child recalls all of the words, further trials need not be undertaken. The examiner should watch for use of subvocalization and other strategies during the reading of the words.

Scoring:
    Use of strategies:
      0 = Absent
      1 = Present

Record the number of trials (1 to 4) needed for the child to master the task as well as the number of words in the best trial (0 to 7).

Interpretation: Children who use strategies well to accomplish new learning tasks generally do well on this task and the one that follows. Semantic clustering techniques often help them remember the stimulus words, for example, linking leg-foot-toe and dog-tree(!) in short-term memory semantic maps. Children who are consistently nonstrategic in their approaches to learning are likely to struggle with the Word Learning task. Difficulty with auditory registration and processing of large chunks as well as attention and cognitive fatigue may compromise performance. Poor performance may be indicative of problems with semantic memory specifically or it may provide further evidence of more generalized trouble with short-term memory (as also reflected on the Pattern Learning and Drawing from Memory tasks).

Pattern Learning

Rationale: This task is analogous to the word learning exercise, but in this case a child is given repeated opportunities to learn a visual pattern. This task requires attention to detail, effective short-term memory, and the ability to register configurations or visual patterns accurately. The correct accomplishment of this task is facilitated through the use of good strategies.

Administration: The child is told: "I am going to show you a whole bunch of boxes with Xs in them. Here they are. I would like you to look at these very carefully, and then I am going to show you some empty boxes. You are going to put Xs in them to make a design that looks just like the one you are studying. I want to see how well you can remember where all the Xs are." The child is given up to 10 seconds to study the pattern. The examiner then hides the stimulus and presents the child with the first set of boxes. The child is asked to put Xs in the right places. If the pattern is imperfect, the examiner shows the child the original design again by placing the *Stimulus Book* over the *Response Book*. After 10 seconds, the stimulus is removed, uncovering the child's previous response and the response boxes below. Four trials are allowed.

Scoring: As in the Word Learning task, the number of trials (0 to 4) is recorded. If the child is unable to master the pattern in four trials, the examiner records the best trial (the number marked correctly less the number marked incorrectly).

Interpretation: Children with weak visual registration and visual processing problems may have difficulty with the visual Pattern Learning task. Again, attention problems and cognitive fatigue may compromise performance. Those with weaknesses of memory for visual gestalt and spatial interrelationships may require multiple trials to master the pattern on the grid. Such children may also have problems in spelling and other activities that demand precise recall of visual patterns. Children may demonstrate a variety of strategies, including the use of their fingers for pointing or tracing in the air and verbal mediation. Children who make good use of such techniques may be more readily amenable to intervention than those who do not.

Motor Sequential Imitation

Rationale: The Motor Sequential Imitation task entails visual sequential registration in short-term memory. The child must be able to appreciate and preserve the serial order as the examiner portrays a particular motor sequence. This activity also stresses sustained attention and keen awareness of directionality. Some children may have difficulty with this task because they are not able to process the examiner's finger movements rapidly enough. This effect can be minimized by offering repeated exposures (unscored) to the original stimuli. Motor sequential memory is likely to be an important requisite for writing (especially cursive) as well as for other fine motor activities that require rapid and precise rhythmic execution, such as learning to use a computer keyboard or play certain musical instruments. Motor sequential memory may also be helpful in enhancing ability with video games.

Administration: For the Motor Sequential Imitation task, the child is asked to hold up both hands with her palms facing the examiner. She is then told to use her dominant hand (which the examiner points to), while the examiner uses the opposite hand. The child is told: "I want you to hold up both of your hands like this. Watch my fingers very carefully. I am going to move my fingers a particular way. I will do it three times and then I want you to do it three times with this hand (point to dominant hand). Be sure that you don't start until I tell you to. Let me show you three times before you start using your fingers." The examiner then proceeds through the various motor sequences as delineated on the *Record Form*. The thumbs should be opposed to each of the other fingers as noted. Each finger contact should last approximately 1 second. The examiner should begin with item 1 and continue until the child has missed two consecutive items. Make sure that the child does each pattern three times. Do not correct the child. However, if the child corrects herself, allow her to pursue three consecutive correct executions.

Scoring:
Individual items:
    0 = Incorrect
    1 = Correct

A score of 1 requires the child to have done the pattern correctly three consecutive times. Record the total number of correct responses (0 to 5).

Interpretation: Deficient motor sequential imitation may be indicative of one or several underlying dysfunctions. Some children have trouble perceiving the actual serial order of the examiner's finger movements because of problems with directionality or with the actual appreciation of sequential order (the latter likely to be reflected on other *PEEX 2* sequencing activities). Poor attention may also impede performance. Most commonly, however, this task is troublesome for children who have problems with motor sequential memory and/or their ability to program a motor output based upon a specific sequential plan. Such gaps are sometimes referred to as motor procedural memory deficits. They may impede cursive writing, keyboarding, and the learning of a musical instrument. It is important to determine whether a child's motor sequential memory problem is part of a more generalized picture of deficient sequential memory as seen on the Digit Spans, Days of the Week, and Hopping in Place tasks or whether it is strictly limited to the fine motor domain.

Visual Processing Functions

The visual processing section of the *PEEX 2* evaluates visual attention, visual discrimination, visual problem solving, and visual motor function. Abilities or inabilities in visual processing may be correlated with performance in writing and spelling as well as with certain aspects of mathematical skill. Weaknesses of visual processing are a relatively *rare* cause of reading problems. Visual processing activities require strengths of attention and also a strategic approach. Therefore, these tasks afford a good opportunity to observe attention and the use of an organized (or disorganized) approach to problem solving. Because the visual processing section is near the end of the *PEEX 2*, one may detect some deterioration in the sustenance of mental effort.

Visual Vigilance

Rationale: The Visual Vigilance task measures sustained attention and continuous performance. The configurations offered are not perceptually complex, but they contain multiple salient details. A superficial or inattentive approach to the task is likely to result in many careless errors. Visual vigilance also involves visual discrimination. Performance on the second item of the task is facilitated through familiarity with letter combinations and phonemes along with experience in discriminating between similar appearing letter symbols (such as *b* and *d*).

Administration: The child is shown the set of designs in the *Response Book*. The examiner points to the stimulus design and says: "If you look at this page, you will see that it has a whole lot of different designs on it. I want you to look carefully at the one that is in the circle. Then I would like you to go through this whole page and put a circle around each design that is *exactly* like the one in the circle, *exactly* like the one I am pointing to. Only circle the ones that are just exactly like it. If you circle one and then change your mind, just put a line through it. Don't bother erasing it. You can start now."

As the child goes through the page, the examiner observes closely, using the grid in the *Record Form*. The circles in the grid represent correct answers. The examiner should put an X in each box that corresponds to one that the child has circled. If the child circles one and then changes his mind, the examiner should simply put lines through the X on the *Record Form*. This provides good documentation of indecision and also of self-monitoring levels. The same procedure is used with the second configuration. The examiner says: "This page has a lot of letters on it. Look at the one in the box (pointing to it). Circle each group of letters that is exactly the same. You can start now."

Scoring: Record the time required to complete the task. Indicate the total number correct and the number of false positives (items circled that should not have been circled). Subtract the number of false positives from the total correct to derive part 1 and part 2 scores.

Use of strategies:
0 = Poor, random, inconsistent, or disorganized approach
1 = Consistent left to right or up and down scanning

Interpretation: Children with attention deficits are the ones most likely to experience problems with the Visual Vigilance task. Poor performance may stem from their inattention and/or impulsivity. Impulsivity is largely revealed in a number of false positive responses, whereas inattention tends to yield omissions of correct matches. Prolonged or very slow performance on these tasks may suggest inefficient visual processing, over-focusing, or visual memory problems (in which case the child needs to keep re-examining the original stimulus). Significantly weaker performance on part 2, which involves letters, compared with part 1, which involves symbols, may indicate students with significant decoding problems in reading. Failure to scan and to use other strategies may suggest generalized problems with planning and organization. The scores indicated as STRATS become part of the summary score for Strategy Use.

Sentence Copying

Rationale: The Sentence Copying task measures several different skills. Successful performance entails effective visual processing, motor speed, prior copying experience, reading skill, and short-term visual memory. The memory component involves the temporary registration of reasonably large chunks of visual-spatial-verbal input. Children with strong decoding skills in reading, good spelling skills, and facility with letter formation are likely to be successful on this task.

Administration: The examiner opens to page 11 in the *Stimulus Book,* which is held 24 inches from the child's face and perpendicular to the table. The child is then told: "I would like you to copy as much as you can from this page. We will take 1 minute and I will tell you when to stop. You don't have to copy everything on the page. Just copy as much as you can in 1 minute. Are you ready? Let's begin." The child then copies the sentence. It is important to observe how frequently she looks up at the original stimulus. Looking up at each letter suggests reading gaps or possible problems with immediate memory for visual gestalts.

Scoring: Record the total number of *complete* words copied (0 to 14). Inaccuracies can be recorded in the spaces in the *Record Form.* See Figure 7 for samples of scoring.

Spacing between words and between letters within words:
0 = More than one spacing error
1 = One spacing error
2 = Consistently good spacing (without error)

Letter formation:
0 = Consistently poor letter formation (more than 5 letters poorly legible or inaccurate)
1 = Inconsistent letter formation (1 to 5 letters poorly legible or inaccurate)
2 = Consistently good letter formation

Accuracy (punctuation, capitalization, omissions, insertions):
0 = Two or more errors
1 = One error
2 = No errors (all details present; no insertions)

Frequency of looking at stimulus:
0 = Looking up at each letter
1 = Looking up at each word
2 = Looking up every two or more words

For *letter formation* the symbols should be fairly well executed, that is, it should be clear what letter the child is forming. Inaccuracies include reversals or other obvious distortions. Letters that are difficult to decipher should be considered illegible. The number of poorly formed or difficult-to-read letters should be added and scored as described above. If the same letter of the alphabet is consistently distorted or malformed each time it appears, it should be scored as one poor letter formation.

The *accuracy* parameter includes errors in copying punctuation and capitalization. For example, the first letter in the sentence and the initial letter of the proper name must be capitalized. If either of these is not, it is scored as an error of accuracy. Other areas of accuracy include insertions of extra words or letters, omissions of specific words or letters, and omissions or insertions of punctuation marks.

Figure 7. The following examples provide suggested scoring for the Sentence Copying task.

While Ben was walking down the street last night, he saw the brown dog.

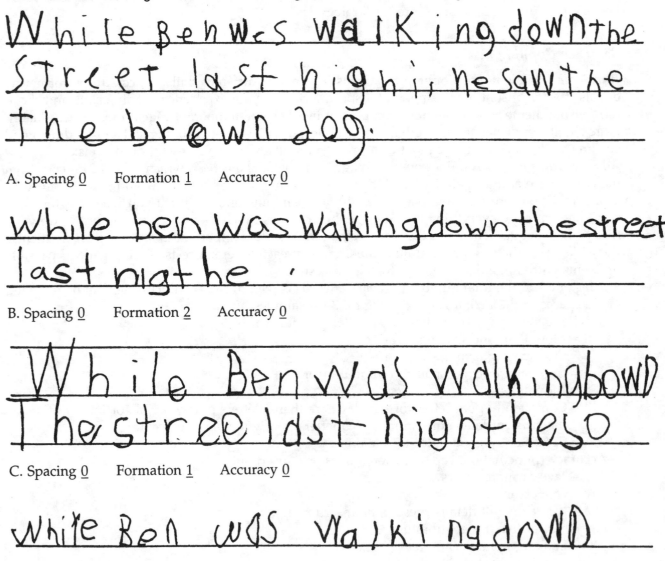

A. Spacing <u>0</u>   Formation <u>1</u>   Accuracy <u>0</u>

B. Spacing <u>0</u>   Formation <u>2</u>   Accuracy <u>0</u>

C. Spacing <u>0</u>   Formation <u>1</u>   Accuracy <u>0</u>

D. Spacing <u>1</u>   Formation <u>1</u>   Accuracy <u>0</u>

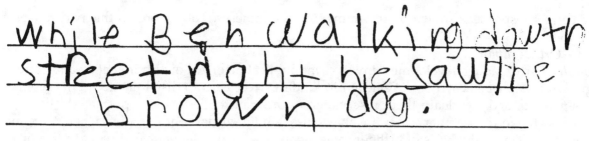

E. Spacing <u>0</u>   Formation <u>1</u>   Accuracy <u>0</u>

F. Spacing <u>0</u>   Formation <u>2</u>   Accuracy <u>1</u>

Interpretation: As the norms show, performance on this task shows obvious developmental progression as literacy skills improve. Poor performance may be associated with major delays in reading and writing. Affected children may be unable to read the sentence, and they may have to laboriously copy letter by letter without decoding the words. Many children struggle on this task because of generalized problems with visual-motor integration or graphomotor dysfunctions. Although they can read the sentence, they have difficulty forming the letters and they therefore write very slowly. Children with visual-spatial problems may show unusual letter formations, reversals, and poor spacing. Many children with attention problems make errors of detail, such as omissions and insertions, and they may experience fatigue and deterioration of letter formation and spelling accuracy over time.

Visual Whole : Part Analysis

Part A — Abstract
Rationale: Whole:part relationships are of great importance for reading, mathematics, and spelling, as well as for other aspects of school. Students are constantly asked to deal with materials where certain parts come together to form a whole story, an entire word, or a visual pattern (as in the identification of a rectangle). In this task, visual whole:part analysis is required. That is, a child needs to determine what goes with what to compose a meaningful unit. This is often accomplished by perceiving parts that go together when they are embedded within nonrelevant elements.
Administration: The child is shown page 12 in the *Response Book* and the examiner says: "We are now going to play a game in which you have to look at a shape and then see if you can find that shape when it is with other things. Let's try this example at the top." The examiner then demonstrates the correct response on the practice stimulus. It is important to show the child that only number 4 is correct. "Although number 3 has the same shape inside, it has been turned around, so it doesn't count. Now try the next one. Remember to find the one that has the shape in it exactly." The child then goes ahead and does all of the others. The examiner should look for signs of impulsivity, poor scanning, and inattention to detail. Also, the use of strategies such as verbal mediation should be noted.
Scoring:
    0 = Incorrect
    1 = Correct

The correct response is shown by the number in parentheses. Total score on this part ranges from 0 to 6.

Part B — Orthography

Rationale: Early reading development involves the application of visual discrimination and pattern recognition to alphabetic symbols. Children in kindergarten learn to discriminate similar letters such as *p* and *d,* and they learn that preservation of order of the letters is important. As they develop a sight word vocabulary, they are able to use familiar visual configurations when decoding and encoding. This is the basis of orthographic awareness. A two-letter search (*pd*) and a word search comprise this task.

Administration: The child is shown page 13 in the *Response Book,* and the *OK* example is pointed out, with the others covered. The examiner says: "Can you find some that look just the same? There are some in here that are hidden. Remember, they have to be in the same order." The examiner allows the child to work on the example. If the child makes an error by circling a vertical, diagonal, or reversed *OK,* the examiner shows the child that they are different. Next *pd* is uncovered, and the examiner says: "Now find all the places where these two letters go together just like this." When the child has finished, the examiner uncovers the word search task and asks the child to find and circle all those words.

Scoring:

Individual items (*pd* or words):

0 = Incorrect

1 = Correct

The *Record Form* includes a grid to facilitate scoring. Total score on Part B ranges from 0 to 12.

Interpretation: Children with visual processing weaknesses, those with attention deficits, and those who have broader difficulties with whole:part relationships are likely to struggle with these challenges. Poor performance on both parts of this task usually indicates visual processing problems, although children with attention deficits may do poorly on these items—especially if they rush through them and produce many impulsive responses. Children with decoding problems in reading are likely to struggle on Part B, especially the word search, but do better on Part A. Tasks such as the one in Part B have been shown to correlate especially highly with spelling accuracy, as poor spellers are apt to have trouble recalling whole:part relationships within words.

Geometric Form Copying

Rationale: The Geometric Form Copying task is, of course, a commonly used test item. It is intended to tap visual-spatial awareness and visual-motor integration. To succeed at this task, children must have a strong appreciation of the interrelationships of parts with a visual pattern. They must focus on fine visual detail while having the ability to survey a whole pattern to reproduce its overall appearance. Form copying also necessitates good pencil control and the ability to reflect and pace oneself.

Administration: The child is told: "Now I would like you to copy some designs for me. I will show you the designs in this book, and I would like you to copy each one as carefully as you can. Take your time and do a very good job." The child is then given four forms to copy, based on age. A six-year-old child does forms 1, 2, 3, and 4; a seven-year-old does forms 3, 4, 5, and 6; and an eight-year-old does forms 5, 6, 7, and 8.

Scoring: Each form is scored for accuracy and pencil control.

Accuracy:

0 = More than one distortion

1 = One distortion

2 = No distortions

More specific scoring criteria for accuracy can be found in Figure 8 (see pages 38–41).
Pencil control:
  0 = More than one line is wavy or poorly executed
  1 = One or no lines are poorly executed
Use of strategies (planning and organization):
  0 = Absent or child appears to proceed impulsively without carefully examining the initial stimulus
  1 = Present

Interpretation: Form copying deficits can be the result of weak visual perceptual abilities, problems with pencil control, or confusion over whole:part relationships. Some children have motor planning problems that make it hard for them to base a motor response on a visual-spatial input. They may also experience trouble copying from the board. Weaknesses of attention (affecting, in particular, attention to visual detail) are a common cause of failure on this task. In fact, it is not unusual for children with attention deficits to be falsely characterized as having visual perceptual difficulties because of their faulty, frenetically executed drawings. Geometric form copying can be severely compromised by impulsivity and a lack of self-monitoring. Often children with attention deficits try to copy the forms so quickly that they omit relevant detail or move their fingers so rapidly that pencil control is compromised and the productions appear messy.

Attention Ratings

Attention Checkpoints 1, 2, and 3 can be added to come up with a total score for all checkpoints on page 15 of the *Record Form*. Also, the total strategy use score is obtained from the sum of the STRATS scores on pages 11, 12, 13, and 14.

Task Analysis

The task analysis pages list the tasks vertically down the left-hand column on both pages in the order in which they are administered. The major constructs (motor functions, language, memory, and visual processing) are shown across the top. Within each of these, the key elemental functions are shown at the bottom of the page. In addition, the last column (general) includes the important functions that do not specifically fit within these broad constructs, that is, attention, planning/organization, rate/rhythmicity, and chunk size. For each task, the relevant elemental functions are shown as unshaded squares. If a child does well on a task (above age norms or relative to his other areas of performance), a plus sign can be placed in each of the unshaded squares for that task. Conversely, performance below the age norms or unexpectedly weak performance can be indicated with a minus sign. The total positive and total negative for each elemental function can then be examined, using the number of items as a denominator. This gives an indication of the extent to which a student's performance suggests strengths and weaknesses across a number of tasks tapping a particular elemental function.

Behavioral Observations

The examiner rates the impressions of the child's adaptation to the examination and affect displayed during the examination. Four parameters are described, including responsiveness, com-

Figure 8. The following illustrations depict the scoring criteria for the Geometric Form Copying task, as well as optimally and imperfectly executed examples of drawings.

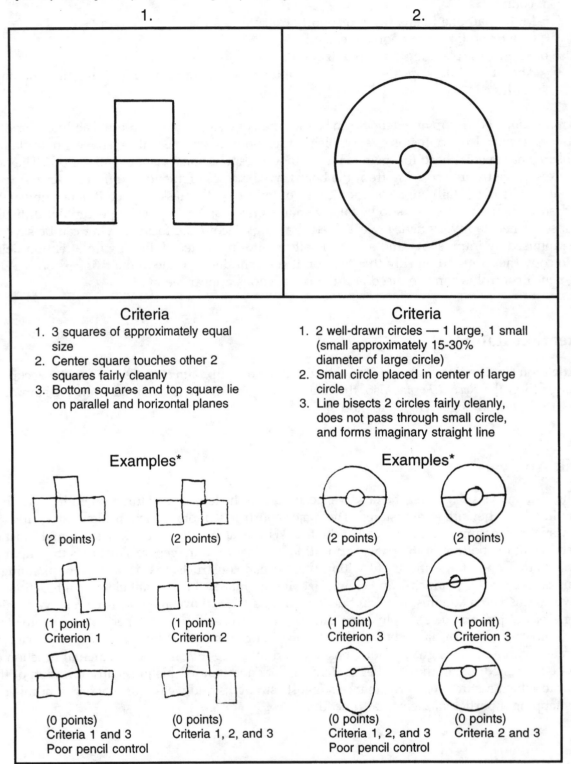

1.

2.

Criteria

1. 3 squares of approximately equal size
2. Center square touches other 2 squares fairly cleanly
3. Bottom squares and top square lie on parallel and horizontal planes

Criteria

1. 2 well-drawn circles — 1 large, 1 small (small approximately 15-30% diameter of large circle)
2. Small circle placed in center of large circle
3. Line bisects 2 circles fairly cleanly, does not pass through small circle, and forms imaginary straight line

Examples*

(2 points)   (2 points)

(1 point)   (1 point)
Criterion 1   Criterion 2

(0 points)   (0 points)
Criteria 1 and 3   Criteria 1, 2, and 3
Poor pencil control

Examples*

(2 points)   (2 points)

(1 point)   (1 point)
Criterion 3   Criterion 3

(0 points)   (0 points)
Criteria 1, 2, and 3   Criteria 2 and 3
Poor pencil control

*Each criterion not met is counted as one distortion.
0 points = More than one distortion
1 point = One distortion
2 points = No distortions

38

3.

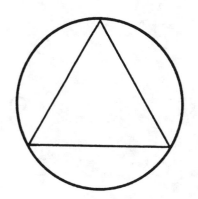

4.

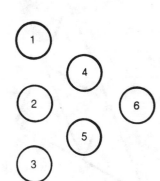

Criteria

1. Triangle occupies more than half of area within circle
2. Triangle intersects circle cleanly at 2 or 3 points
3. Triangle is equilateral, or nearly so

Criteria

1. Six circles, fairly equally spaced
2. Circles 1, 2, 3 form straight line and circles 2, 6 form straight line perpendicular to line of 1, 2, 3

3. Orientation of circles approximates equilateral triangle

Examples*

(2 points)

(1 point)
Criterion 3

(1 point)
Criterion 3

(1 point)
Criterion 2

(0 points)
Criteria 2 and 3
Poor pencil control

(0 points)
Criteria 2 and 3
Poor pencil control

Examples*

(2 points)

(2 points)

(1 point)
Criterion 1

(1 point)
Criterion 1

(0 points)
Criteria 1, 2, and 3

(0 points)
Criteria 1, 2, and 3
Poor pencil control

5.

6.

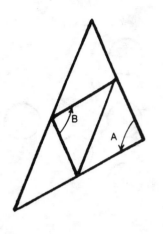

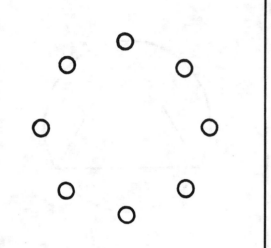

Criteria

1. Two triangles (longer hypotenuse on left, shorter on right)
2. At least two corners of inner triangle cleanly touch approximate midpoints of lines forming outer triangle
3. Angles A and B are approximately 90° angles

Criteria

1. Eight circles drawn
2. Not more than one circle falls outside generally circular pattern
3. Fairly regular spacing between circles

Examples*

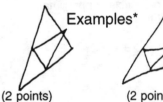

(2 points)

(2 points)

(1 point)
Criterion 1
Poor pencil control

(0 points)
Criteria 2 and 3

(0 points)
Criteria 1, 2, and 3

(0 points)
Criteria 1, 2, and 3
Poor pencil control

Examples*

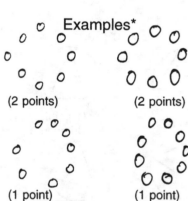

(2 points)

(2 points)

(1 point)
Criterion 3

(1 point)
Criterion 1

(0 points)
Criteria 2 and 3

(0 points)
Criteria 2 and 3

*Each criterion not met is counted as one distortion.
0 points = More than one distortion
1 point = One distortion
2 points = No distortions

7. **8.**

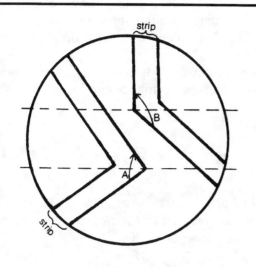 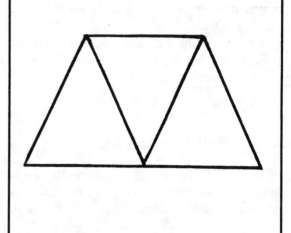

Criteria

1. Outer circle well drawn
2. Imaginary lines drawn parallel through angles A and B divide circle into approximately 3 equal parts
3. Lines forming strips are approximately parallel

Criteria

1. 3 triangles of approximately equal size
2. Base and top are parallel
3. Triangles share common sides

Examples*

(2 points) (2 points)

(2 points)

(1 point)
Criterion 3

(1 point)
Criterion 2

(1 point)
Criterion 1

(1 point)
Criterion 3

(0 points)
Criteria 1 and 3
Poor pencil control

(0 points)
Criteria 2 and 3

(0 points)
Criteria 1 and 3
Poor pencil control

(0 points)
Criteria 1 and 2
Poor pencil control

pliance, self-confidence, and rapport with the examiner. These ratings may indicate that a child exhibits inordinate performance anxiety, that he has trouble relating to others, or that there are indications of oppositional behavior. In interpreting test results, it is important to know how cooperative the child was during the procedure. Obviously a youngster who is withdrawn or noncompliant may perform suboptimally on the *PEEX 2* as a consequence of difficulties adapting to the examination.

The Behavioral Observations page also provides an opportunity to record a child's affect. Excessive anxiety or an unusual range of mood can interfere with performance and/or have implications for future counseling needs.

General Health Assessment

The General Health Assessment consists of a routine physical examination as well as neurological and sensory assessments. On the *PEEX 2* this is an integral part of the neurodevelopmental examination, generally conducted after the neurodevelopmental testing.

Summary Impressions

The Summary Impressions page (*Record Form*, page 20) provides an opportunity for the examiner to compile a general overview of the child. While this should not replace a more detailed account of performance, it can be useful in generating a brief summary or in quickly reviewing a case prior to seeing a child for a follow-up visit. There is no specific scoring system for this grid. However, Table 2 indicates which test items are likely to be most germane to the categories of function or health listed in Summary Impressions.

Conclusion

More than anything else, the *Pediatric Early Elementary Examination 2* is intended to help us understand children and the conditions they face as they strive to be successful in school. In particular, it is meant to help us interpret the struggles of young children who are experiencing too much failure too early in life. By integrating findings on the *PEEX 2* with other sources of information about such children, we can create highly specific profiles of their neurodevelopmental strengths and weaknesses, profiles that go well beyond the traditional labels, thereby enabling the adult world to respond supportively and with compassion. The derived profiles are important because they permit schools, clinicians, parents, and the children themselves to collaborate to implement forms of educational care that will foster success for individual children—each through the pursuit of his or her unique pathways. It is hoped that the *PEEX 2* will enable clinicians to play a most meaningful role in this vital process.

TABLE 2

Area	Major Items to Consider
Fine Motor Function	Imitative Finger Movement Finger Tapping Pencil Control Pencil Speed Write Alphabet Imitate Gestures Motor Sequential Imitation Sentence Copying Geometric Form Copying
Graphomotor Function	Pencil Control Pencil Speed Write Alphabet Graphomotor Observation Grid
Receptive Language	Phonological Awareness (Parts A, B, and C) Sentence Repetition Complex Sentences Verbal Instructions Paragraph Summarization and Comprehension Word Learning Informal observations of response to directions
Expressive Language	Phonological Awareness (Parts A, B, and C) Picture Naming Sentence Formulation Paragraph Summarization Word Learning Informal observations during examination
Gross Motor Function	Sustained Motor Stance Rapid Alternating Movement Hopping in Place Sidewise Tandem Gait Catch Ball
Memory	Write Alphabet Phonological Awareness (Parts A and C) Picture Naming Sentence Repetition Verbal Instructions Paragraph Summarization and Comprehension Digit Spans Drawing from Memory Days of the Week Word Learning Pattern Learning Motor Sequential Imitation Sentence Copying

Area	Major Items to Consider
Sequencing	Finger Tapping Write Alphabet Phonological Awareness (Parts B and C) Paragraph Summarization Rapid Alternating Movement Hopping in Place Digit Spans Days of the Week Motor Sequential Imitation
Visual Processing	Imitative Finger Movement Imitate Gestures Picture Naming Verbal Instructions Catch Ball Drawing from Memory Pattern Learning Motor Sequential Imitation Visual Vigilance Sentence Copying Visual Whole:Part Analysis Geometric Form Copying
Attention	Attention Ratings (Summary) Visual Vigilance
Higher-Order Cognition	Paragraph Comprehension Visual Whole:Part Analysis Total Strategies Score
Affect	Behavioral Observations
Behavior	Behavioral Observations
Strategy Use	Total Strategies Score
Minor Neurological Indicators	Lateral Preference (mixed/incomplete dominance) Imitative Finger Movement (finger agnosia) Sustained Motor Stance (motor impersistence, spooning, choreiform twitches) Rapid Alternating Movement (dysdiadochokinesis) Sidewise Tandem Gait (dystonic posturing) Total Associated Movements Score
Neurological Findings	General Health Assessment
Physical Health	General Health Assessment
Growth/Maturation	General Health Assessment

Appendix

The following pages offer a prototype of a completed *PEEX 2 Record Form* and *Response Book*. Study of these materials will help clarify specific points about scoring and documentation of findings. For those who wish to check their reliability as raters, a videotape* of this particular case is available from Educators Publishing Service. The reader can view the tape and score it using a blank *PEEX 2 Record Form*, which can then be compared to the sample in this manual.

The following is a brief synopsis of the background history of the child whose *PEEX 2* results are depicted on these pages.

Trent is an 8-year-old boy who recently completed the second grade at a public elementary school. His first- and second-grade teachers have had concerns about him, as he has had great difficulty acquiring skills in reading and arithmetic. He has been delayed in developing sound-symbol associations for reading, although toward the end of second grade he began to make rapid progress in this area. He has made fewer gains in arithmetic, where he still experiences difficulty with basic counting skills and understanding concepts. His second-grade teacher believed that Trent did make good progress in written output and spelling, although his performance in these areas remained somewhat deficient compared to his classmates'.

Trent has not been a behavior problem in school or at home. He has managed to maintain his self-esteem and academic motivation despite his difficulties. However, there have been concerns about his attention. Trent is moderately distractible and fidgety; this is especially true when he needs to engage in sustained listening in school. His parents also observe attention weaknesses at home.

Trent appears to relate well to other children. He is a highly competent athlete—especially in baseball. His parents report that Trent is very effective at expressing himself verbally and that he has many good ideas and insights. He has a strong interest in science and social studies.

Trent has always been in good health with the exception of recurrent ear infections. PE tubes were inserted on two occasions. He underwent a tonsillectomy and adenoidectomy. He has had no other surgical procedures or hospitalizations. There has been no history of seizures, head trauma, or any chronic illness.

All of Trent's early developmental milestones were appropriate. However, he had great difficulty learning to tie his shoelaces. Trent attended a preschool and was not reported to have any problems with learning or behavioral adjustment at that time.

Trent has been receiving stimulant medication for his attention; this treatment has been somewhat helpful to him. Trent did not take medication on the day of the testing reported on these forms.

*The videotape was made as part of a postgraduate course for professionals on August 3, 1995, in Raleigh, North Carolina.

PEDIATRIC EARLY ELEMENTARY EXAMINATION

Peex 2
Record Form

developed under the direction of
Mel Levine, MD, FAAP

from The Division of Ambulatory Pediatrics,
The Children's Hospital, Boston, MA

further developed by Mel Levine, MD, and Adrian D. Sandler, MD, at the Clinical Center for the Study of Development and Learning,* University of North Carolina at Chapel Hill, and supported in part by a grant from the Robert Wood Johnson Foundation.

Printed in U.S.A.   ISBN 0-8388-2805-6
July 1995 printing

*The CDL is a University Affiliated Program

Patient's/Student's Name: **Trent**
Code number
Date: **8/13/95**
☐ Clinic ☐ Office ☐ School ☒ Other
Examiner: **Levine**

I.D. Number: _____
Examiner: _____
Grade (next grade, if summer): **0**
Sex (1 = female; 2 = male): **2**
Age: years **8**
months **7**
Parents present (0=neither; 1=one; 2=two): **2**

Age Key
- 6-0 to 6-11
- 7-0 to 7-11
- (8-0 to 8-11)

FINE MOTOR/GRAPHOMOTOR FUNCTIONS

Lateral Preference
		Dominance
Hand preference (pencil–ball–hammer–teeth) (0=mixed; 1=L; 2=R)	(0–2)	2
Eye preference (3 trials) (0=mixed; 1=L; 2=R)	(0–2)	1

Imitative Finger Movement (examiner holds position)

Somesthetic input / Visual-motor integration / Attention / Visual registration

R.H.: Single (1–2)(1–4)(1–3)(1–5)	Number correct	(0–4) 4	AM*
Synkinesia—left hand		(0,1)	AM
L.H.: Single (1–3)(1–2)(1–4)(1–5)	Number correct	(0–4) 3	
Synkinesia—right hand		(0,1)	
Total correct (RH plus LH)	Total correct	(0–8) 1 0	AM
Visual monitoring (0=present; 1=absent)		(0,1)	
Hesitancy/false starts (0=>2; 1=≤2)		(0,1)	
Impulsivity		(0,1)	

Finger Tapping (index finger, 20 taps on table)

Motor speed / Motor sequencing / Rate

Dominant hand taps (right ☒ left ☐)	Trial 1	(0,1) 1 1	AM
	Trial 2	(0,1) 1 1	AM
	Time (seconds)	(0,1) 1 1	
Associated movement (mouth)			
Synkinesia			
Dyskinesia/Dysmetria			
Non-dominant hand taps	Trial 1	(0,1) 1 1	AM
	Trial 2	(0,1)	AM
	Time (seconds)	(0,1)	
Associated movement (mouth)			
Synkinesia			
Dyskinesia/Dysmetria			

Pencil Control (untimed)

Eye-hand coordination / Graphomotor control / Attention / Visual motor integration

Number of contacts (Form A)	Contacts A	8 4	AM
Number of contacts (Form B)	Contacts B		
	Total contacts (A+B)	10	
Associated movement (mouth)		(0,1)	
Impulsivity		(0,1)	

Pencil Speed (15 seconds)

Eye-hand coordination / Graphomotor control / Motor speed / Rate

Total units completed		(0–15) 10	
Total Intersections		10	
Units minus intersections	Corrected total	0 0	AM
Associated movement (mouth)		(0,1)	

*Associated movement key: 0=present; 1=absent

Total Correct
6	4–7
7	5–8
8	7–8

Seconds
6	5–8
7	5–7
8	5–7

Seconds
6	6–9
7	5–8
8	5–8

Total Contacts
6	3–8
7	2–5
8	2–3

Corrected Total
6	4–7
7	6–9
8	6–10

ATTENTION CHECKPOINT ONE (Fine Motor/Graphomotor)

OBSERVATION	SCORE			DESCRIPTION
Impulsivity	0	1	(2)	Started task in an unplanned manner or answered too quickly—compromising quality
Frenetic tempo	0	1	(2)	Paced task too quickly
Poor attention to detail	0	1	(2)	Missed relevant detail during task
Distractibility	0	1	(2)	Became distracted during task or seemed not to listen
Mental fatigue	0	1	(2)	Yawned, stretched, otherwise showed fatigue during task
Deterioration over time	0	1	(2)	Lost focus as task progressed or had difficulty sustaining attention
Performance inconsistency	0	1	(2)	Showed erratic error pattern during task
Poor monitoring	0	1	(2)	Performance impaired by poor monitoring or made careless errors
Gross overactivity	0	1	(2)	Displayed extraneous large muscle motion during task, e.g., appeared restless, left seat
Fidgetiness	0	1	(2)	Displayed extraneous small muscle motion during task, e.g., appeared fidgety, squirmy

Total for Checkpoint One (0–20) 2 0

Total	
6	16–20
7	19–20
8	19–20

Key
0=observed on >1 task   1=observed on 1 task
2=never observed

Comments: *Was well focused*

Paced self well

FINE MOTOR/GRAPHOMOTOR FUNCTIONS

Write Alphabet* (60 seconds—lowercase manuscript)

Handedness (0=left; 1=right)	Motor speed	(0,1)	1
Number of letters written (E=5, J=10, O=15, T=20) Total number	Motor memory / Motor sequencing / Graphomotor control	(0–26)	1 4
Reversals (0=present; 1=none)	Sequential memory	(0,1)	0
Letter formations (0=all poorly formed; 1=some poorly formed; 2=all well formed)	Retrieval	(0–2)	2
Letter sequence (0=letters transposed, omitted, inserted; 1=appropriate sequence)	Rate	(0,1)	1
Associated movement (mouth)		(0,1)	1 AM

*Complete Graphomotor Observation Grid below.

Imitate Gestures
(0=errors/unable; 1=difficult, slow; 2=quickly and correctly)

Interlocking rings	Eye-hand coordination / Praxis / Visual processing functions / Attention	(0–2)	2
Rectangle		(0–2)	0
Bat		(0–2)	0
Horse		(0–2)	2
Total score		(0–8)	4 AM
Synkinesia		(0,1)	1
Associated movement and synkinesia subtotal		(0–10)	1 0

Total Score	
6	6–7
7	6–8
8	7–8

Graphomotor Observation Grid

Check one: cursive □   mixed □   manuscript ☒

OBSERVATION	0	1	2	SCORE		
SPEED OF OUTPUT	Notably slow	Inconsistent	Appropriate	(0)	1	2
FLUENCY/RHYTHMICITY OF OUTPUT	Marked hesitancy	Some hesitancy	Smooth flow	(0)	1	2
STABILIZATION OF PAPER	Non-writing hand never used	Inconsistent	Well stabilized by both hands	0	1	(2)
CONSISTENCY OF GRIP	Not at all established	Somewhat variable	Consistent	(0)	1	2
DISTANCE FROM FINGER TO POINT	1/2 inch or less	Inconsistent	Approximately 3/4 to 1 inch	(0)	1	2
PRESSURE ON PENCIL	Markedly increased	Moderately increased	Normal	0	(1)	2
ANGLE OF PENCIL	Close to perpendicular	Inconsistent angle	Approximately 45° with page	0	(1)	2
POSITION OF WRIST	Hooked (flexed >20°)	Somewhat flexed	Normal (slight extension)	0	(1)	2
POSITION OF THUMB	Thumb over two fingers	Forefinger-thumb contact	Forefinger-thumb opposed	0	(1)	2
MOVEMENT OF JOINTS	Mainly wrist movement	Mainly proximal* finger joints	Mainly distal* finger joints	0	(1)	2
DISTANCE FROM EYES TO PAPER	<3 inches	3–5 inches	>5 inches	0	1	(2)

*Proximal = third (larger) joints; Distal = first two (smaller) joints

Total graphomotor observation score (0–22) 1 0

LANGUAGE FUNCTIONS

Picture Naming

Record **exact** errors and circumlocutions next to stimulus words. Circle H for hesitations and C for circumlocutions.
(0=incorrect; 1=correct)

	Phonology
	Word retrieval
	Semantics
	Expressive fluency
	Visual pattern recognition
	Rate

#	Word		Score
1.	Duck	(0,1) H C	1
2.	Lamp	(0,1) H C	1
3.	Screw	(0,1) H C	0
4.	Pan	(0,1) H C	1
5.	Brush	(0,1) H C	1
6.	Thermometer	(0,1) H C	1
7.	Spider	(0,1) H C	1
8.	Rocket	(0,1) H C	1
9.	Giraffe	(0,1) H C	1
10.	Guitar	(0,1) H C	1
11.	Ruler	(0,1) H C	1
12.	Wheel	(0,1) H C	1
13.	Umbrella	(0,1) H C	1
14.	Bench	(0,1) H C	0
15.	Triangle	(0,1) H C	1
16.	Shelves, Bookcase	(0,1) H C	1
17.	Jar	(0,1) H C	1
18.	Socks	(0,1) H C	1
19.	Windmill *(OK with phonetic cue)*	(0,1) H C	0
20.	Chicken *(OK with phonetic cue)*	(0,1) H C	0

Time (seconds) (0-20)   0 4 9
Total correct (0-2)   1 6 / 2

Seconds	
6	26-63
7	26-55
8	21-45

Total Correct	
6	14-19
7	16-19
8	17-20

Articulation (0=abnormal on >1 item; 1=normal)

After administration of entire task under timed conditions, examiner may assess whether child is more successful on missed items with semantic cues ☐ or phonemic cues ☒

Sentence Repetition (Document errors in texts of sentences)

	Sentence comprehension
	Syntax
	Attention
	Memory functions
	Chunk size

2=no errors
1=one error; preserved syntax and meaning
0=two or more errors/lost meaning

#	Sentence		Score
1.	The girls climbed the tall tree.	(0-2)	2
2.	Will Billy wear his new red coat?	(0-2)	2
3.	The girl did not like the boy who lived down the street.	(0-2)	2
4.	The children wanted to go swimming, even though it was still raining.	(0-2)	2
5.	Bob can't go to the ball game until he changes his shoes.	(0-2)	2
*6.	After they finished eating dinner, they went to the movie.	(0-2)	0

Total score (0-12)   0.9

Articulation (0=abnormal on >1 word; 1=normal)   1

Total Score	
6	8-11
7	10-12
8	10-12

* *Two trials — couldn't repeat it*

LANGUAGE FUNCTIONS

Phonological Awareness

	Phonology
	Semantics
	Attention
	Auditory registration

Part A — Rhyming
(Example: Lick-Stick)

1. Hot   _top_   — Total correct (20 seconds)   1
   — Total phonological errors   0
   — Total non-words   1
2. Rake   — Total correct (20 seconds)   0
   — Total phonological errors   0
   — Total non-words   0

Total correct (1+2)   0.2

Total Correct (1+2)	
6	3-10
7	4-10
8	5-10

Part B — Phoneme Segmentation
(Example: Take has 3 sounds. How many sounds in *luck?* Demonstrate.)
(0=incorrect; 1=correct)

#	Word		Score
1.	Bike (3)	(0,1)	1
2.	Steam (4)	(0,1)	0
3.	Paper (4)	(0,1)	0
4.	Soup (3)	(0,1)	1
5.	Go (2)	(0,1)	1
6.	Shout (3)	(0,1)	1
7.	Silly (4)	(0,1)	0
8.	Goose (3)	(0,1)	1

Total correct (0-8)   5

Total Correct	
6	2-6
7	4-6
8	4-6

Part C — Deletion and Substitution
(Example: If you change the /m/ sound in *moose* to /g/, you get *goose*. How about /b/ in *bat* to /h/?)
(0=incorrect; 1=correct)

#	Item		Score
1.	b in Bake to t (take)	(0,1)	1
2.	l in Look to c (cook)	(0,1)	1
3.	f in Fan to t (tan)	(0,1)	0
4.	p in Pit to n (nit)	(0,1)	0
5.	h in Hail to j (jail)	(0,1)	0
6.	s in Soup to l (loop)	(0,1)	0

Total correct (0-6)   2

Total Correct	
6	2-4
7	2-6
8	4-6

LANGUAGE FUNCTIONS

Sentence Formulation

	Used Word (0,1)	Grammar (0,1)	Complete Sentence (not run-on) (0,1)	Meaningful (0,1)		Semantics	Syntax
							Expressive fluency
							Semantics
							Syntax
							Planning/organization
							Rate
1. Book DK	0	0	0	0			
2. Made	1	1	1	1			
3. Before DK	0	0	0	0			
4. If DK	0	0	0	0			
5. Water Who ✗	✗	0	0	0			
6. Very But	—	—	—	—			

Total score (0–24) 4

Impulsivity (0=impulsive; 1=appropriate) (0,1) 1

*Ease of production/fluency (0–2) 0

*0=considerable hesitancy; >1 false start; prolonged effort
1=some hesitancy; false start
2=no hesitancy; quick response

Total Score	
6	12–22
7	18–24
8	21–24

Record sentences (optional)

1. (would not attempt)
2. I made a cake.
3. (would not attempt)
4. (would not attempt)
5. (would not attempt)
6. (not administered)

LANGUAGE FUNCTIONS

Complex Sentences
(0=incorrect; 1=correct)

			Semantics
			Sentence comprehension
			Syntax
			Attention
			Auditory registration
1. The car is parked next to the garage. Where is the car parked? *(near)*	Next to garage	(0,1)	0
2. Before the door was opened, the boy put his coat on. *Rep.* When did the boy put his coat on?	Before door opened	(0,1)	0
3. The boy who liked the girl ran away down the street. Who ran away down the street?	Boy	(0,1)	0
4. The lion that the tiger bit jumped over the giraffe. Who jumped over the giraffe?	Lion	(0,1)	1
5. The horse jumped over the fence after it started raining. *When* When did the horse jump over the fence?	*After* it started raining	(0,1)	0
6. The girl saw the man who was wearing green shoes. Who was wearing green shoes?	Man	(0,1)	1
7. The clown who called the little dog ran into the tent. Who ran into the tent?	Clown	(0,1)	0
8. The car that was hit by the truck was driven by the man. What did the man drive?	Car	(0,1)	0

Total correct (0–8) 2

Total Correct	
6	4–5
7	5–6
8	6–7

Verbal Instructions
(Document errors below.)
(0=Incorrect; 1=correct)

		Sentence comprehension
		Syntax
		Attention
		Chunk size
		Memory functions
		Visual processing functions
1. Touch the middle square with your pencil and then with your finger.	(0,1)	1
2. Touch the small square and the large circles with your pencil.	(0,1)	0
3. Put a circle around one of the small X's.	(0,1)	1
4. Draw lines under the big square and the little one.	(0,1)	1
5. Make a dot in the big square or the middle one.	(0,1)	0
Rep. 6. Before you make an X in a big circle, put a dot underneath it.	(0,1)	0
7. When I point to the smallest square, put an X under a small circle. **(Wait 5 seconds; point to a small circle; then large square; then smallest square.)**	(0,1)	0
8. If the big square is under the little square, make a circle at the bottom of the page. *Rep.*	(0,1)	0
9. Touch the middle square with your pencil and then with your finger.	(0,1)	1
10. Touch the small square and the large circles with your pencil.	(0,1)	0

Total score (0–10) 0.5

Total Score	
6	5–6
7	6–8
8	7–9

ATTENTION CHECKPOINT TWO (Language)

OBSERVATION	SCORE			DESCRIPTION
Impulsivity	0	1	(2)	Started task in an unplanned manner or answered too quickly—compromising quality
Frenetic tempo	0	1	(2)	Paced task too quickly
Poor attention to detail	(0)	1	2	Missed relevant detail during task
Distractibility	0	(1)	2	Became distracted during task or seemed not to listen
Mental fatigue	0	1	(2)	Yawned, stretched, otherwise showed fatigue during task
Deterioration over time	(0)	1	2	Lost focus as task progressed or had difficulty sustaining attention
Performance inconsistency	(0)	1	2	Showed erratic error pattern during task
Poor monitoring	0	1	(2)	Performance impaired by poor monitoring or made careless errors
Gross overactivity	0	1	(2)	Displayed extraneous large muscle motion during task, e.g., appeared restless, left seat
Fidgetiness	0	(1)	2	Displayed extraneous small muscle motion during task, e.g., appeared fidgety, squirmy

Total for Checkpoint Two (0–20) _12_

Key
0=observed on >1 task   1=observed on 1 task
2=never observed

Comments: _Had trouble maintaining auditory attention on multiple tasks_

Total	
6	12–19
7	14–20
8	14–20

LANGUAGE FUNCTIONS

Paragraph Summarization and Comprehension

Ages 6 to 7-11

Passage A (Experiential/Narrative Form)

It was a hot day. Mary's mother gave her some money and asked her to go to the store and buy some ice cream. On the way home Mary stopped to talk with a friend. When she got home, the bag was dripping. Mary was worried. She knew her mother would be angry.

Summarization: _Repeated—still could not summarize_

1. It was a hot day. (0,1)
2. Mother gave her money. (0,1)
3. She went to the store/bought some ice cream. (0,1)
4. On the way home Mary stopped to talk with a friend. (0,1)
5. Bag was dripping. (0,1)
6. Mary was worried. (0,1)
7. She knew her mother would be angry. (0,1)
8. Sequence (0=poor; 1=appropriate) (0,1)

Summarization score (0–8)

NOTE: Administered after B.

Comprehension and recall:
1. What was the weather like? (Hot) (0,1)
2. What did Mary's mother ask her to do? (Go to the store/buy some ice cream) (0,1)
3. Why did Mary stop on the way home? (To talk to a friend.) (0,1)
4. Why was the bag dripping? (The ice cream melted.) (0,1)
5. How did Mary feel? (Worried) (0,1)
6. Why was she worried? (She knew her mother would be angry.) (0,1)

Comprehension score (0–6)

Sentence comprehension	
Discourse processing	
Summarization	
Expressive fluency	
Attention	
Memory functions	
Chunk size	

Summarization	
6	3–6
7	5–7

Comprehension	
6	2–4
7	3–6

Ages 8 to 8-11

Passage B (Decontextualized/Expository Form—Causal Chain)

A long time ago horses were brought to America from Spain to work on farms and ranches. Many of these horses escaped. They formed large herds and were so tough they were able to survive on just small amounts of grass and water. After a while there were millions of them. Today in some parts of the American West, these wild horses are crowded together. This is causing big problems for them. Many are now very thin and unhealthy.

Summarization:
1. Wild horses were brought to America. (0,1)
2. Many horses escaped. (0,1)
3. Horses could survive on small amounts of water and grass. (0,1)
4. After a while there were millions of them. (0,1)
5. Now they are crowded together/unhealthy/thin. (0,1)
   (0 = all details omitted; 1 = one or more details included)
6. Organization (0 = poor; 1 = appropriate) (0,1)

Summarization score (0–6)

Comprehension and recall:
1. Why were the wild horses first brought to America? (To work on farms/ranches) (0,1)
2. What did many horses do after they arrived in America? (Escaped) (0,1)
3. How were the escaped horses able to survive in the wild? (They could survive on small amounts of grass and water) (0,1)
4. Where are these horses now found? (The American West) (0,1)
5. What problems are many of these horses now having? (Too crowded/unhealthy/thin) (0 = missed all details; 1 = included one or more details) (0,1)
6. Why are the horses getting so thin? (Not enough food/grass) (0,1)

Comprehension score (0–6)

Summarization	
8	3–5

Comprehension	
8	3–4

MEMORY FUNCTIONS

Digit Spans

(If correct, record 1 in right-hand column; if incorrect, record a zero and document the actual response in the left-hand column.)

		Auditory registration
		Short-term memory
		Sequential memory
		Attention
		Chunk size

Start:	7 9 2	—
	3 8 6	—
	4 1 3	—
	9 6 1 5	1
3	3 8 7 2	0
	5 3 7 4	1
7	7 1 6 4 3	0
4	9 2 5 8 4	0
	2 9 7 1 6	—
	3 6 5 2 1	—
	8 3 1 7 9 6	—
	4 7 2 5 1 8	—

Maximum length of span with 2 correct ... Span (3–6) **4**
Strategy use (e.g., subvocalization) (0,1) **0**

STRATS*

	Span
6	4
7	4–5
8	4–5

Drawing from Memory

(Deduct one point from any drawing containing additional/extraneous detail.)

		Short-term memory
		Visual registration
		Attention
		Visual processing functions
		Chunk size
		Planning/organization

1. Vertical and diagonal lines (each one point) (0–2) **0**
2. Dot and inverted T (each one point) (0–2) **1**
3. r and q (each one point) (0–2) **1**
4. 9 and 6 (each one point) (0–2) **0**
5. Outer rectangle (one point)
   Two vertical lines (each one point)
   Horizontal line (one point)
   Small vertical (one point)
   Integrated (not blocks) (one point)
   Proportions (one point) (0–7) **2**

Total score (0–15) **4**
Correct drawings (0–5) **0**
Strategy use (e.g., rehearsal, imaging, subvocalization, verbal mediation) (0,1) **0**

STRATS

	Total Score
6	6–10
7	10–14
8	10–14

*Strategy use key: 0=absent; 1=present

GROSS MOTOR FUNCTIONS

Sustained Motor Stance (15 seconds)
(0=present; 1=absent)

		Somesthetic input
		Vestibular function
		Motor inhibition

Impersistence (<15 secs.) (0,1)
Choreiform twitches (tongue) (0,1)
Choreiform twitches (fingers) (0,1)
Spooning (fingers) (0,1)

Rapid Alternating Movement (10 seconds)

		Somesthetic input
		Praxis
		Motor sequencing
		Motor inhibition

Dominant side (right ☒ left ☐) Rhythmicity (0–1)
Quality (0=poor; 1=good) (0,1)   AM
Proximal inhibition (0=present; 1=absent) (0,1)   AM
Synkinesia (0,1)   AM
Associated movement (mouth) (0,1)

Non-Dominant Side
Quality (0=poor; 1=good) (0–1)
Proximal inhibition (0,1)   AM
Synkinesia (0,1)   AM
Associated movement (mouth) (0,1)   AM

Hopping in Place (twice on each foot for 10 seconds)

		Motor sequencing
		Motor inhibition
		Motor memory
		Praxis
		Rhythmicity

Quality (0=poor; 1=variable; 2=good) (0–2) **2**
Dystonic posturing (0=present; 1=absent) (0,1)

Sidewise Tandem Gait (10 feet)

		Somesthetic input
		Vestibular function
		Praxis
		Visual processing functions

Quality (0=poor; 1=variable; 2=good) (0–2) **2**
Dyskinesia (0=present; 1=absent) (0,1)
Dystonic posturing (0,1)

Catch Ball (10 feet, both hands, six tries after two practice trials)

		Eye-hand coordination
		Praxis
		Visual-spatial awareness

Successful catches (0–6) **6**

Associated movement and synkinesia subtotal (0–6) **6**
Associated movement total (see pp. 2 and 10) (0–16) **16**

	Total Catches
6	3–5
7	4–6
8	5–6

	Total Associated Movements
6	8–14
7	9–15
8	11–15

VISUAL PROCESSING FUNCTIONS

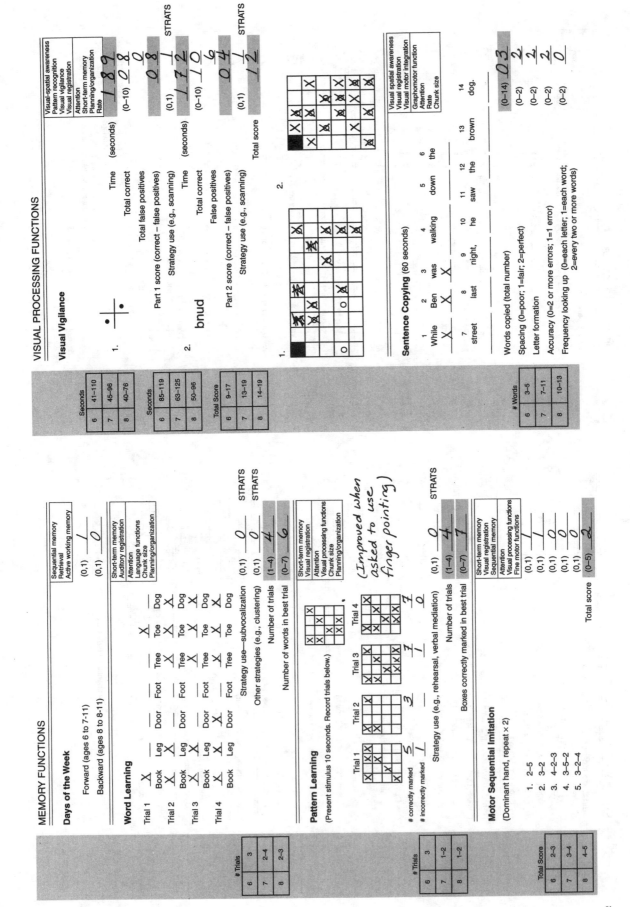

Visual Vigilance

	Visual-spatial awareness
	Pattern recognition
	Visual vigilance
	Visual registration
	Attention
	Short-term memory
	Planning/organization
	Rate

1.

Time (seconds) (0–10) 1 8 9 ___ 0 8
Total correct (0,1) 0
Total false positives (0,1) 0 8
Part 1 score (correct – false positives) 1
Strategy use (e.g., scanning) 2 2 — STRATS

2. **bnud**

Time (seconds) (0–10) 1 1 0 ___ 0 6
Total correct (0,1) 0 4
False positives 1
Part 2 score (correct – false positives) 1 2 — STRATS
Strategy use (e.g., scanning)

Total score

	Seconds
6	41–110
7	45–96
8	40–76

	Seconds
6	85–119
7	63–125
8	50–96

	Total Score
6	9–17
7	13–19
8	14–19

Sentence Copying (60 seconds)

1	2	3	4	5	6
While	Ben	was	walking	down	the
X	X	X			

7	8	9	10	11	12	13	14
street	last	night,	he	saw	the	brown	dog.

	Visual spatial awareness
	Visual registration
	Visual motor integration
	Graphomotor function
	Attention
	Rate
	Chunk size

Words copied (total number) (0–14) 0 3
Spacing (0=poor; 1=fair; 2=perfect) (0–2) 2
Letter formation (0–2) 2
Accuracy (0=2 or more errors; 1=1 error) (0–2) 2
Frequency looking up (0=each letter; 1=each word; 2=every two or more words) (0–2) 0

	# Words
6	3–5
7	7–11
8	10–13

MEMORY FUNCTIONS

Days of the Week

	Sequential memory
	Retrieval
	Active working memory

Forward (ages 6 to 7-11) (0,1) 1
Backward (ages 8 to 8-11) (0,1) 0

Word Learning

Trial 1	Book	Leg	Door	Foot	Tree	Toe	Dog
	X	X				X	X
Trial 2	Book	Leg	Door	Foot	Tree	Toe	Dog
	X	X			X	X	X
Trial 3	Book	Leg	Door	Foot	Tree	Toe	Dog
	X	X			X		X
Trial 4	Book	Leg	Door	Foot	Tree	Toe	Dog

	Short-term memory
	Auditory registration
	Attention
	Language functions
	Chunk size
	Planning/organization

Strategy use—subvocalization (0,1) 0 — STRATS
Other strategies (e.g., clustering) (0,1) 0 — STRATS
Number of trials (1–4) 4
Number of words in best trial (0–7) 6

	# Trials
6	3
7	2–4
8	2–3

Pattern Learning
(Present stimulus 10 seconds. Record trials below.)

Trial 1   Trial 2   Trial 3   Trial 4

	Short-term memory
	Visual registration
	Attention
	Visual processing functions
	Chunk size
	Planning/organization

(Improved when asked to use finger pointing)

Strategy use (e.g., rehearsal, verbal mediation) (0,1) 0 — STRATS
Number of trials (1–4) 4
Boxes correctly marked in best trial (0–7) 7

correctly marked: 5 (Trial 1), 3 (Trial 2), 1 (Trial 3), 7 (Trial 4)
incorrectly marked: 1 (Trial 1), — (Trial 2), 1 (Trial 3), 0 (Trial 4)

	# Trials
6	3
7	1–2
8	1–2

Motor Sequential Imitation
(Dominant hand, repeat × 2)

	Short-term memory
	Visual registration
	Sequential memory
	Attention
	Visual processing functions
	Fine motor functions

1. 2–5 (0,1) 1
2. 3–2 (0,1) 0
3. 4–2–3 (0,1) 0
4. 3–5–2 (0,1) 0
5. 3–2–4

Total score (0–5) 2

	Total Score
6	2–3
7	3–4
8	4–5

ATTENTION CHECKPOINT THREE (Visual Processing)

OBSERVATION	SCORE	DESCRIPTION
Impulsivity	0 1 (2)	Started task in an unplanned manner or answered too quickly—compromising quality
Frenetic tempo	0 1 (2)	Paced task too quickly
Poor attention to detail	0 1 (2)	Missed relevant detail during task
Distractibility	0 1 (2)	Became distracted during task or seemed not to listen
Mental fatigue	0 1 (2)	Yawned, stretched, otherwise showed fatigue during task
Deterioration over time	0 1 (2)	Lost focus as task progressed or had difficulty sustaining attention
Performance inconsistency	0 1 (2)	Showed erratic error pattern during task
Poor monitoring	0 1 (2)	Performance impaired by poor monitoring or made careless errors
Gross overactivity	0 1 (2)	Displayed extraneous large muscle motion during task, e.g., appeared restless, left seat
Fidgetiness	0 1 (2)	Displayed extraneous small muscle motion during task, e.g., appeared fidgety, squirmy

Total for Checkpoint Three (0-20): **20**

Total	
6	11-18
7	16-20
8	16-20

Key
0=observed on >1 task
1=observed on 1 task
2=never observed

Attention strong with visual inputs

Attention Ratings (summary)

Checkpoint One (page 3—Fine Motor/Graphomotor) (0-20)	20
Checkpoint Two (page 9—Language) (0-20)	12
Checkpoint Three (page 15—Visual Processing) (0-20)	20
Total (all checkpoints) (0-60)	52
Strategy use (Total STRATS score) (0-10)	03

See pages 11-14.

Total Score	
6	39-57
7	50-60
8	45-60

Strategy Use	
6	3-7
7	4-8
8	5-8

Comments: *Very inconsistent attention at Checkpoint 2—particularly on tasks involving language and memory. Attention strong visually! (was nonstrategic in approach to tasks)*

VISUAL PROCESSING FUNCTIONS

Visual Whole : Part Analysis

Part A: Abstract (N.B.: Rotations are incorrect)

(Visual-spatial awareness / Visual problem solving / Pattern recognition / Attention)

1. (4) (0,1): 1
2. (1) (0,1): 1
3. (3) (0,1): 1
4. (2) (0,1): 1
5. (3) (0,1): 0
6. (2) (0,1): 0

Total (0-6): **4**

Part B: Orthography (N.B.: Changes in order and/or orientation of letters are incorrect.)

1. pd (0-4): 4
2. (0-8): 5

Very slow, strong attention

Total (0-12): **09**

Strategy use (scanning) (0,1): 1 — STRATS
Strategy use—other (e.g., verbal mediation, subvocalization) (0,1): 0 — STRATS

Total	
6	3-5
7	5-6
8	5-6

Total	
6	9-12
7	11-12
8	11-12

Geometric Form Copying

(Visual motor integration / Visual-spatial awareness / Attention / Planning/organization / Fine motor functions)

Age	Form	Accuracy* (0-2)	Pencil Control (0,1)	Fine motor functions (0-3)
6	Form 1			1.
6	Form 2			2.
6-7	Form 3	2	1	3. 3
6-7	Form 4	2	1	4. 3
7-8	Form 5	0	0	5. 0
7-8	Form 6	0	0	6. 0
8	Form 7			7. 0
8	Form 8			8. 0
	Total Score			

Total score (0-12): **06**

Strategy use—planning and organization (0,1): 0 — STRATS

Total Score	
6	5-11
7	7-11
8	7-12

*(0=>1 distortion; 1=1 distortion; 2=no distortions)

TASK ANALYSIS

Motor Functions / Language (page 16)

Tasks	Motor Functions									Language							
	Eye-hand coordination	Motor inhibition	Motor speed	Praxis	Motor memory	Motor sequencing	Vestibular function	Somesthetic input	Graphomotor control	Phonology	Semantics	Syntax	Word retrieval	Sentence comprehension	Discourse processing	Summarization	Expressive fluency
Lateral preference																	
Imitative finger movement																	
Finger tapping																	
Pencil control																	
Pencil speed																	
Write alphabet																	
Imitate gestures																	
Phonological awareness																	
Picture naming																	
Sentence repetition																	
Complex sentences																	
Verbal instructions																	
Sentence formulation																	
Paragraph summarization/comprehension																	
Sustained motor stance																	
Rapid alternating movement																	
Hopping in place																	
Sidewise tandem gait																	
Catch ball																	
Digit spans																	
Drawing from memory																	
Days of the week																	
Word learning																	
Pattern learning																	
Motor sequential imitation																	
Visual vigilance																	
Sentence copying																	
Visual whole-part analysis																	
Geometric form copying																	
Total Positive	0	0	0	0	0	0	0	0	0	0	0	0	0	0	0	0	0
Total Negative	5	3	4	2	2	3	3	0	5	2	5	4	2	4	1	1	2
Number of Items	6	3	4	6	3	5	2	4	5	2	5	4	2	4	1	1	3

Memory / Visual Processing / General (page 17)

Tasks	Memory						Visual Processing						General			
	Auditory registration	Visual registration	Short-term memory	Sequential memory	Active working memory	Retrieval	Dominance	Visual-motor integration	Visual vigilance	Visual-spatial awareness	Visual pattern recognition	Visual problem solving	Attention	Planning/Organization	Rate/Rhythmicity	Chunk size
Lateral preference																
Imitative finger movement																
Finger tapping																
Pencil control																
Pencil speed																
Write alphabet																
Imitate gestures																
Phonological awareness																
Picture naming																
Sentence repetition																
Complex sentences																
Verbal instructions																
Sentence formulation																
Paragraph summarization/comprehension																
Sustained motor stance																
Rapid alternating movement																
Hopping in place																
Sidewise tandem gait																
Catch ball																
Digit spans																
Drawing from memory																
Days of the week																
Word learning																
Pattern learning																
Motor sequential imitation																
Visual vigilance																
Sentence copying																
Visual whole-part analysis																
Geometric form copying																
Total Positive	0	0	0	0	0	0	0	0	0	0	0	0	0	0	0	0
Total Negative	5	5	7	7	3	3	3	7	2	8	2	2	14	4	6	7
Number of Items	6	6	9	4	3	3	1	9	3	11	3	3	17	6	9	8

GENERAL HEALTH ASSESSMENT

Height _____ ins ☐   Weight _____ lbs. ☐   Head Circumference _____ ins ☐

Blood Pressure _____ / _____ ☐   General Appearance _____ ☐ ☐

Vision (Specify Test _____)   ☐

Hearing (Specify Method _____)   ☐

(Place an x in the box to the left of any abnormal findings. Cross out items not performed.)

☐ Hair and Scalp	☐ Heart—Murmurs	☐ Sensation
☐ Skin	☐ Abdomen/Appearance	☐ Other Neurological
☐ Eyes—Fundoscopic	☐ Abdomen—Masses	☐ Urinalysis
☐ Eyes—Oculomotor	☐ Genitalia—Hernia	☐ Hemoglobin/Hematocrit
☐ Eyes—Other	☐ Genitalia—Other	☐ Other Items, Tests:
☐ Ears—Tympanic Membranes	☐ Anorectal	
☐ Ears—Canals	☐ Lymph Nodes	
☐ Ears—Other	☐ Extremities—Joints	
☐ Nasopharynx	☐ Extremities—Muscles	
☐ Oropharynx	☐ Extremities—Other	Immunizations (Date Completed)
☐ Mouth—Teeth, Gums	☐ Vertebral Column	Dt _____ Measles _____ Mumps _____
☐ Mouth—Other	☐ Cranial Nerves	Polio _____ Rubella _____ Tb _____
☐ Neck—Palpation	☐ Reflex Intensity	Other(s)
☐ Chest—Appearance	☐ Reflex Symmetry	
☐ Lungs—Auscultation	☐ Pathological Reflexes	
☐ Heart—Rhythm, Rate	☐ Gait	

Summary of Findings and Overall Health:

_____

_____

_____

Relevant Health History:

_____

_____

_____

Examiner _____   Date _____

BEHAVIORAL OBSERVATIONS

ADAPTATION TO EXAMINATION

	0	1	2
Responsiveness	Never warmed up	(1) Took some time to warm up	2 Was immediately engaged
Compliance	Often resistant to demands or directions	1 Sometimes resistant to demands or directions	(2) Cooperative; easily accepted directions
Self-confidence	Needed constant support or reassurance	(1) Sometimes needed reassurance	2 Self-reliant; no reassurance required
Rapport with examiner	Never formed alliance or related to examiner	1 Had some difficulty forming alliance or relating to examiner	(2) Readily formed alliance or related to examiner

AFFECT

	0	1	2
Anxiety	Exhibited fear and/or anxiety throughout testing session	(1) Somewhat anxious or slow to overcome anxiety	2 Exhibited no anxiety
Affective range	Blunted; flat affect	(1) Somewhat blunted affect	2 Appropriately varied
Affective stability	Widely fluctuating affect (e.g., laughing, tearful)	1 Somewhat labile affect	(2) Consistent affect
Verbal spontaneity	Taciturn; never initiated communication	(1) Sometimes initiated communication	2 Communicative; spontaneous

Comments: *Slightly anxious; somewhat quiet but cooperative and interested*

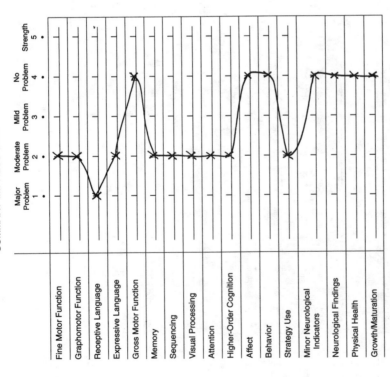

EXAMINER'S NOTES*

1. Moderate problems with attention — inconsistent focus — mainly with auditory/language inputs.

2. Significant language delays — phonological, sentence, and discourse levels — receptive and expressive.

3. Slow rate of processing

4. Gross motor strengths

5. Some evidence of inconsistent memory function

*This page provides space for the examiner to make notes about the child and family that may be helpful in demystification, family discussion, or report writing.

SUMMARY IMPRESSIONS*

	Major Problem 1	Moderate Problem 2	Mild Problem 3	No Problem 4	Strength 5
Fine Motor Function					
Graphomotor Function					
Receptive Language					
Expressive Language					
Gross Motor Function					
Memory					
Sequencing					
Visual Processing					
Attention					
Higher-Order Cognition					
Affect					
Behavior					
Strategy Use					
Minor Neurological Indicators					
Neurological Findings					
Physical Health					
Growth/Maturation					

Additional concerns/Strengths/Stylistic observations:

Overall difficulties mainly with attention, memory, language

*This page provides space for the examiner to record summary impressions and qualitative observations based on the child's performance. There is no specific scoring system for this grid.

Trent

Peex 2

Response Book

developed under the direction of
Melvin D. Levine, MD, FAAP

from The Division of Ambulatory Pediatrics,
The Children's Hospital, Boston, MA

further developed by Melvin D. Levine, MD,
and Adrian D. Sandler, MD, at the Clinical Center
for the Study of Development and Learning,*
University of North Carolina at Chapel Hill, and
supported in part by a grant from the Robert
Wood Johnson Foundation.

Printed in U.S.A.   ISBN 0-8388-2808-6

*The CDL is a University Affiliated Program

PENCIL CONTROL

Start ➡

A

Start ➡

B

PENCIL SPEED

1 2 3 4 5 6 7 8 9 10 11 12 13 14 15

➡ Start

WRITE ALPHABET

a b c d e f g h i j k l m n

1

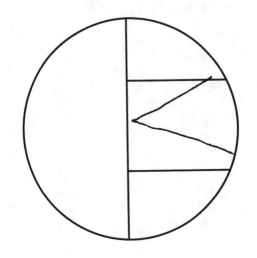

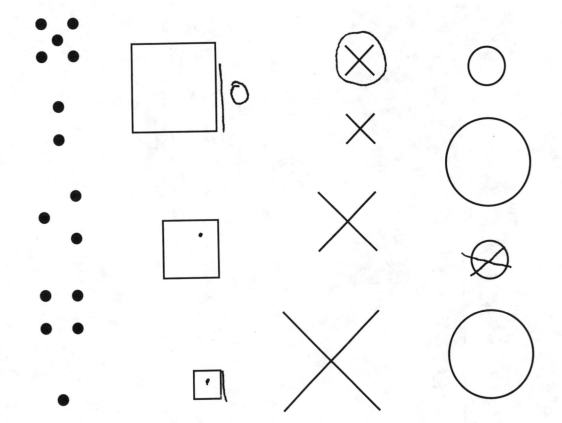

gp ơ u

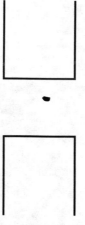

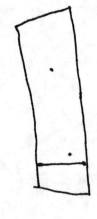

17 4 3

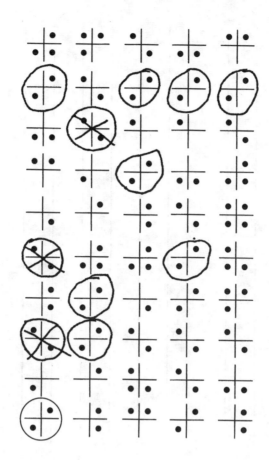

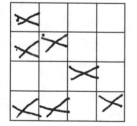 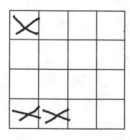 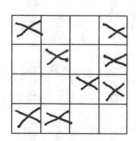 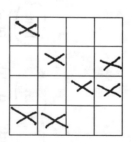

While Ben was wa

bnud | bund | dnub | bund | bnud | bnud
bund | bund | bnud | bnud | bnud | dnud
bnud | bnud | dunb | bnud | bund | bnud
bund | bund | bnud | bdun | bund | bund
bnud | bund | dnud | bund | dnud | bnud

PART B

Example

| o k |

p o k r t
o n k x o
k o b o k
s r k o t
b l o k a

1.

| p d |

a f r p d
b p k r l
p d f d p
n p b p d
l n p d r

2.

| the |
| me |
| to |
| on |
| off |
| cat |
| dog |
| red |

e f a p d o g r
o t b o n t h e r
c a m e b l r o
n o s d h t e r
p c a t n a m b
t l o f f b o g
k o b n r e d s
n t o b p l a t

PART A

Example

1.

2.

3.

4.

5.

6.

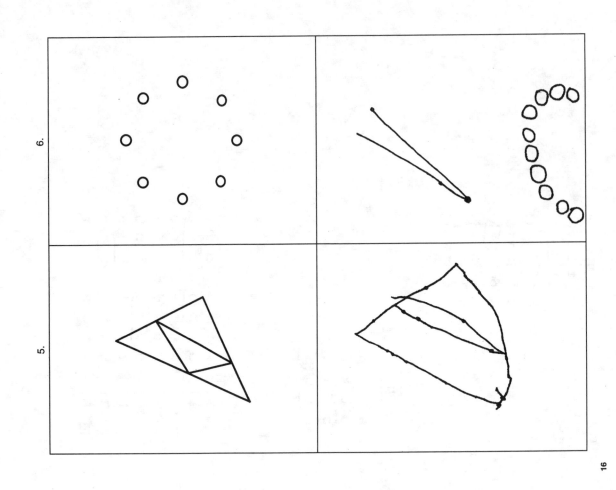

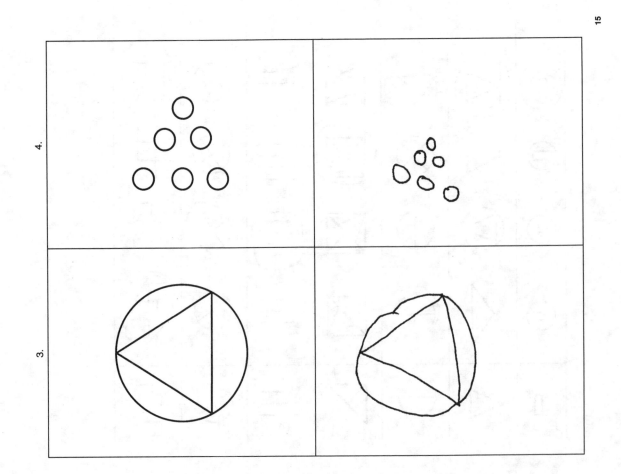

References

Kenny, T., Gaes, G., Saylor, W., et al. The pediatric early elementary examination: sensitivity and specificity. *Journal of Pediatric Psychology* 15:21–26, 1990.

Levine, M.D. *Developmental Variation and Learning Disorders.* Cambridge, Mass.: Educators Publishing Service, Inc., 1987.

Levine, M.D. *Educational Care.* Cambridge, Mass.: Educators Publishing Service, Inc., 1994.

Levine, M.D. *The Pediatric Early Elementary Examination. Examiner's Manual.* Cambridge, Mass.: Educators Publishing Service, Inc., 1983.

Levine, M.D., Sandler, A.D. *The Pediatric Examination of Educational Readiness at Middle Childhood 2. Examiner's Manual.* Cambridge, Mass.: Educators Publishing Service, Inc., 1996.

Levine, M.D., Hooper, S., Montgomery, J., et al. Learning disabilities: an interactive developmental paradigm. In Lyon, G.R., Gray, D.B., Kavanagh, G.J., Krasnegor, N.A., eds., *Better Understanding Learning Disabilities.* Baltimore: Paul H. Brookes, 229–250, 1993.

Levine, M.D., Meltzer, L.J., Busch, B., et al. The pediatric early elementary examination: studies of a neurodevelopmental examination for seven- to nine-year-old children. *Pediatrics* 71:894–903, 1983.

Levine, M.D., Rappaport, L., Fenton, T., et al. Neurodevelopmental readiness for adolescence: studies of an assessment instrument for 9- to 14-year-old children. *Journal of Developmental and Behavioral Pediatrics* 9:181–188, 1988.

Sandler, A.D., Hooper, S.R., Levine, M.D., et al. The pediatric examination of educational readiness at middle childhood (PEERAMID): factor structure and criterion-related validity in a clinic-referred sample of children and adolescents. *Children's Hospital Quarterly* 5 (1):19–26, 1993.

Sandler, A.D., Hooper, S.R., Watson, T.E., et al. Talkative children: verbal fluency as a marker for problematic peer relationships in clinic-referred children with attention deficits. *Perceptual and Motor Skills* 76:943–951, 1993.

Sandler, A.D., Watson, T.E., Footo, M., et al. Neurodevelopmental study of writing disorders in middle childhood. *Journal of Developmental and Behavioral Pediatrics* 13:17–23, 1992.